24 Fundraising Trends & Predictions for 2024

Jeremy Reis

24 Fundraising Trends & Predictions for 2024 © 2024 Jeremy Reis

Nonprofit Donor Press

Resources: http://nonprofitfundraising.com/2024trends

All rights reserved. No part of this book may be reproduced or utilized in any form or by any means, electronic or mechanical, or by any information storage and retrieval system—except for brief quotations for the purpose of review, without written permission from the publisher.

Printed in the United States of America.

Limit of Liability / Disclaimer of Warranty: While the publisher and author have used their best efforts in preparing this book, they make no representations or warranties with respect to the accuracy or completeness of the contents of this book and specifically disclaim any implied warranties of merchantability or fitness for a particular purpose. No warranty may be created or extended by sales representatives or written sales materials. The advice and strategies contained herein may not be suitable for your situation. You should consult with a professional where appropriate. This book was written by Jeremy Reis in his personal capacity. The opinions expressed in this book are the author's own and do not reflect the view of the CRISTA Ministries. Neither the publisher nor author shall be liable for any loss of profit or any other commercial damages, including but not limited to special, incidental, consequential, or other damages. Readers should be aware that Internet Web sites offered as citations and/or sources for further information may have changed or disappeared between the time this was written and when it is read.

We need your help ...

As we step into the new year, the landscape of nonprofit fundraising is not just evolving; it's undergoing a transformative shift. In this book, we explore the 24 most compelling  fundraising trends and predictions for 2024, each offering a unique insight into the future of philanthropy and donor engagement. These insights, carefully curated and analyzed, are designed to equip you with the knowledge and tools you need to navigate this ever-changing terrain.

However, the future of fundraising is shaped not just by trends and forecasts but by the collective experiences and insights of those at the forefront of this dynamic field. This is where your valuable contribution comes into play. We recognize that the wisdom within these pages is just a starting point, and the real story of fundraising in 2024 is still being written – by people like you.

We warmly invite you to be a part of this ongoing narrative. If you have observed a trend, made a prediction, or have an insightful story about fundraising that you believe should be shared, we encourage you to contribute. Whether it's a fresh strategy that's yielding results, a technological innovation changing the way donations are made, or a new approach to donor engagement, your experiences are the lifeblood of our collective understanding.

To share your insights, please visit https://nonprofitfundraising.com/2024trends. Here, you can submit your own trends or predictions, and be a part of shaping the future of fundraising. Every submission is a valuable piece of the larger puzzle, helping to create a comprehensive, up-to-date picture of where fundraising is headed in 2024 and beyond.

By contributing, not only do you add to the richness of this resource, but you also join a community of forward-thinking professionals and enthusiasts who are collectively pushing the boundaries of what's possible in nonprofit fundraising. Together, we can create a future for philanthropy that is as dynamic and diverse as the world it seeks to support.

Let's shape the narrative of nonprofit fundraising in 2024 with each shared insight and prediction. Your voice matters, and we can't wait to hear it.

Table of Contents

Introduction 1

Part 1: Donor-Centric Strategies 11

    Trend 1: Increases in Non-Cash Giving 17

    Trend 2: Gen X and Millennial Importance 27

    Trend 3: Emphasis on Donor Experience 35

    Trend 4: Hyper-Personalized Communications 45

    Trend 5: Peer-to-Peer Fundraising 53

    Trend 6: Reimagining Fundraising Events 61

Part 2: Tech-Powered Fundraising 69

    Trend 7: AI Integration in Fundraising Tools 75

    Trend 8: Investment in Owned Media 83

    Trend 9: Growing Significance of Marketing Automation 91

    Trend 10: Prediction: TikTok Launches Charity Marketplace 99

    Trend 11: Use of Interactive and Gamified Fundraising 105

Part 3: Community & Collaboration 111

    Trend 12: Global Collaboration and Fundraising 115

    Trend 13: Cause-Related Marketing Partnerships 121

    Trend 14: Rise of Social Media Influencers in Fundraising 127

    Trend 15: Adoption of Subscription Model Donations 133

Part 4: Impact & Accountability 141

    Trend 16: Increased Focus on Donor Privacy 145

Trend 17: Transparent Impact Reporting 151

Trend 18: Increased Regulation and Compliance 157

Part 5: Macro Trends 163

Trend 19: Impact of Presidential Elections 167

Trend 20: Decline in Church Attendance Affecting Giving 173

Trend 21: Mergers & Consolidations 179

Trend 22: Protests & Increase in 'Rage Giving' 189

Trend 23: Shift Grant Funding to Localization 195

Trend 24: Staff Turnover 201

End Notes 210

Introduction

2024 is going to be a challenging year. This probably comes as no surprise to you, and considering the last few years, probably comes with a little fear for what might happen.

It's clear that 2024 will be a transformative year, one that promises as many challenges as it does opportunities. It's in this context of change and uncertainty that this book was born, out of a desire to not just navigate the year ahead but to embrace it with confidence and foresight.

I wrote this book with a singular mission in mind: present a path for nonprofit leaders as we venture into a landscape that is evolving more rapidly than ever before. The year 2024 is not just another year; it's a prompt to adapt, innovate, and think ahead. The stakes are high, and the pace of change is relentless, but therein lies the opportunity – the chance to redefine the way we engage with our donors, to elevate our impact, and to forge a future that is as sustainable as it is visionary.

In these pages, you'll find a distillation of the most pertinent trends and predictions for 2024, each accompanied by actionable strategies designed for you and your organization to chart a course through the year. This is a handbook that has the latest research, frontline experiences, and insights from nonprofit leaders.

Whether you're a seasoned fundraiser or just starting your journey in the nonprofit sector, this book is for you. It's for the strategists seeking direction, the visionaries looking for validation, and the pragmatists in search of practical solutions. Together, we'll unpack the complexities of the year ahead, turning predictions into plans, and I pray for your organization, challenges into triumphs.

Let's move into 2024 with the knowledge that though the path is unchartered, we have a guide that we can use to shape the journey.

The Evolving Landscape of Fundraising

Nonprofit fundraising has never been static, but the pace and magnitude of change we've witnessed in recent years is unprecedented.

Technological Advancements: A Double-Edged Sword

The advent of technology has been a double-edged sword, offering incredible tools and simultaneously setting new standards and expectations. The digital revolution has democratized access to information and networks, enabling even the smallest nonprofits to reach global audiences. Social media, AI, and data analytics have emerged not just as tools, but as integral components of our fundraising strategies, helping us understand and engage with donors in ways that were once beyond our imagination. However, with these advancements come challenges – the need for constant upskilling, the pressure to keep up with the ever-changing digital landscape, and concerns around data privacy and security.

Societal Shifts: Redefining Donor Expectations

Societal shifts have left an indelible mark on the fundraising landscape. The rise of social consciousness, especially among younger generations, has led to donors not just giving but seeking to make an impact through their contributions. Donors today *expect* transparency, engagement, and proof of impact. They are no longer content with being passive benefactors; they want to be active participants in the causes they support. This shift demands a new approach to fundraising – one that is more collaborative, more inclusive, and more focused on creating a shared sense of purpose and impact.

Economic Changes: Navigating Uncertainty

Economic fluctuations have always influenced donor behavior, but recent global events, including the pandemic and geopolitical tensions, have introduced a new level of uncertainty. This uncertainty affects not just the availability of funds but also influences donor priorities and the stability of long-term commitments. Nonprofits have had to adapt quickly, finding new ways to sustain operations, engage donors, and deliver on their missions amidst these economic shifts.

While the traditional methods of fundraising are being challenged, the fundamentals of fundraising don't change.

Though technology may change, though we may live through a challenging political climate, and though donor behavior may shift, we are still called to be resilient leaders.

Understanding and Adapting: The Lifeline of Success

The ability to understand and adapt to new trends is what keeps nonprofit organizations relevant. It's about more than just keeping up; it's about anticipating changes and being ready to pivot strategies effectively and efficiently. When nonprofits embrace innovation, whether in technology, donor engagement, or fundraising methods, they not only sustain their operations but also enhance their impact. Adapting to new trends allows organizations to connect with donors in more meaningful ways, tap into new funding streams, and stand out in a crowded and competitive landscape.

Adaptation also means being proactive in addressing challenges and turning them into opportunities. It involves a willingness to learn, to experiment, and sometimes, to take calculated risks. For example, though 2024 may be a financially challenging year, we're still investing significantly in donor acquisition at World Concern. We're testing new channels and trying new campaigns. Organizations that cultivate a culture of adaptability are better positioned to navigate uncertainties and seize the opportunities that arise from change.

The Risks of Not Keeping Pace

The risks of not keeping pace with changes in the fundraising landscape are significant and multi-faceted. Organizations that cling to outdated methods may find themselves struggling to engage modern donors who expect transparency, personalization, and technological savvy in their interactions. This can lead to a decline in donor retention and difficulty in attracting new supporters, ultimately impacting the organization's financial health and its ability to fulfill its mission.

Furthermore, failing to adapt can leave organizations vulnerable to external shocks, such as economic downturns or shifts in donor priorities. In a landscape where change is the only constant, flexibility and agility are not just assets; they are safeguards against unpredictability.

Finally, organizations that do not evolve risk losing their relevance. In a world where social issues and donor preferences are continuously evolving, nonprofits must remain attuned to these shifts to maintain their connection with the community and their supporters. Stagnation can lead to a loss of trust and credibility, making it harder to mobilize support when it is most needed.

What to Expect

This book is a comprehensive guide, a collection of insights and strategies designed to navigate the challenges and opportunities of nonprofit fundraising in 2024. Here's a snapshot of what you can expect:

Donor-Centric Strategies

This book delves deep into the art of understanding and engaging donors. We'll explore innovative approaches to non-cash giving, the growing significance of Generations X and Millennials, and the ever-important emphasis on donor experience. Trends on hyper-personalized communications and the evolving nature of peer-to-peer fundraising will provide you with the tools to create more meaningful and enduring relationships with your supporters.

Tech-Powered Fundraising

Technology is reshaping the fundraising arena. This book will guide you through the integration of AI in fundraising tools, the strategic investment in owned media, and the evolving landscape of marketing automation. With a special focus on emerging platforms like TikTok and the use of interactive and gamified approaches, these trends will equip you to leverage technology in innovative ways.

Community & Collaboration

Understanding the power of collaboration, this book highlights the importance of global partnerships, cause-related marketing, and the influential role of social media influencers. We will also explore the adoption of subscription model donations, showcasing how collaboration can extend beyond traditional boundaries to create lasting impact.

Impact & Accountability

In an era where transparency and accountability are paramount, this book emphasizes the need for clear impact reporting and compliance with increasing regulations. We'll explore the challenges and lessons from celebrity-founded charities and provide insights into maintaining donor trust and credibility.

Macro Trends

No book on fundraising predictions would be complete without examining the broader macro trends. We'll discuss the implications of presidential elections, the impact of declining church attendance, the increasing trend of mergers and consolidations, and fundraising staff turnover. Additionally, we'll tackle the sensitive topics of 'rage giving' to political groups, protests, and the shift of space grant funding towards more localized efforts.

Rest assured, each trend in this book goes beyond theory. You'll find actionable insights, real-world examples, and practical strategies tailored to help you navigate the complexities of fundraising in 2024. Whether you're planning to refine your current practices or overhaul your strategy completely, this book is designed to be a valuable, hands-on resource for you and your organization. Let's turn these predictions into your success stories.

Part 1: Donor-Centric Strategies

Developing donor-centric fundraising strategies isn't a new trend. For many nonprofit organizations, it's the cornerstone to their success. However, there are several trends that we believe will require your organization to invest in the donor experience. This section is dedicated to bringing you closer to your donors, understanding their motivations, and crafting experiences that resonate with them on a deeper level. Here's what you can look forward to learning in the first six trends.

Trend 1: Increases in Non-Cash Giving

The landscape of giving is changing, and non-cash contributions are at the forefront of this transformation. In this trend, we'll explore the rising trend of non-cash donations, including stocks, real estate, and other assets.

Boomers are retiring and the biggest asset transfer in history is happening over the next decade. You'll learn how to identify potential non-cash donors, effectively communicate the benefits of non-cash giving, and navigate the logistical and legal complexities that come with these types of donations. Practical case studies will provide insights into how leading nonprofits are capitalizing on this trend to fuel their missions.

Trend 2: GenX and Millennial Importance

Generations X and Millennials are becoming increasingly significant in the philanthropic world. This trend surveys the values, communication preferences, and giving patterns of these pivotal generations. We'll explore strategies for engaging these donors through technology, storytelling, and impact-driven experiences. You'll learn how to tailor your messaging, create meaningful interactions, and cultivate long-term relationships with these essential donor segments.

Trend 3: Emphasis on Donor Experience

Donor experience is the linchpin of sustained engagement and giving. This trend focuses on creating a seamless, personalized donor journey. We'll cover the principles of excellent donor service, from the first touchpoint to ongoing engagement. You'll learn techniques for gathering and utilizing donor feedback, personalizing communication, and making every donor feel valued and understood. Real-world examples will illustrate how a stellar donor experience can boost retention rates and transform one-time givers into lifelong supporters.

Trend 4: Hyper-Personalized Communications

In a world cluttered with information, personalization is key to cutting through the noise. This trend dives into the art and science of hyper-personalized communications. Leveraging data, AI, and an understanding of donor behavior, you'll learn how to craft messages that speak directly to the individual interests and motivations of your donors. We'll explore tools and techniques for segmenting your audience, automating personalized outreach, and measuring the effectiveness of your communication strategies.

Trend 5: Peer-to-Peer Fundraising

Peer-to-peer fundraising is evolving, and this trend will keep you on the cutting edge. We'll explore the latest trends in peer-to-peer campaigns, including the use of social media, gamification, and influencer partnerships. You'll learn how to empower your supporters to become advocates for your cause, creating a ripple effect that expands your reach and amplifies your impact. Case studies will highlight innovative peer-to-peer campaigns that have captivated audiences and driven significant results.

Trend 6: Reimagining Fundraising Events

Fundraising events are a staple of nonprofit strategies, but the playbook is being rewritten. This trend focuses on reimagining these events for a new era. From virtual gatherings to hybrid experiences, you'll learn how to design events that captivate your audience, convey your mission, and drive donations. We'll discuss how to leverage technology, create immersive experiences, and ensure that every event is an unforgettable journey that deepens donor engagement.

In Part 1 of this book, you'll gain a wealth of knowledge and practical strategies to enhance your donor-centric approach. Each trend is designed to build upon the last, creating a comprehensive framework that will elevate your understanding of your donors and refine your engagement strategies. By focusing on the preferences, experiences, and motivations of your donors, you'll not only meet your fundraising goals but also foster a community of dedicated supporters who are invested in the success of your mission.

As you progress through these trends, remember that being donor-centric is an ongoing journey. It requires attentiveness, adaptability, and a willingness to continuously learn and evolve. With the insights and strategies provided in this section, you'll be well-equipped to navigate the complexities of modern fundraising and create meaningful connections that resonate with your donors and drive your organization forward.

Trend 1: Increases in Non-Cash Giving

The greatest wealth transfer in history has begun. And much of that transfer will be in non-cash assets such as stocks, real estate, businesses, and other valuables. Tax implications will present opportunities to nonprofit organizations to receive non-cash gifts in 2024.

Non-cash giving is the donation of assets other than cash to nonprofit organizations. This type of giving encompasses a wide range of assets, including stocks, bonds, real estate, artwork, and other valuable items. Unlike traditional cash donations, non-cash contributions offer donors an alternative means to support their chosen causes, often with added tax benefits and without directly impacting their liquid capital.

For nonprofits, accepting non-cash gifts opens doors to substantial new funding sources, enabling them to diversify their revenue streams and potentially tap into larger donations that reflect a significant portion of the donor's wealth. This form of giving represents a shift in donation strategies, aligning with the evolving nature of wealth and providing an avenue for more impactful philanthropy.

The landscape of American wealth is heavily skewed towards non-cash assets. Astonishingly, about 90% of the nation's wealth is tied up in non-cash assets, ranging from stocks and real estate to valuable collectibles. Despite this, a disproportionate 80% of charitable giving occurs in cash.[i] This discrepancy points to a significant untapped potential for non-cash contributions, an area that is ripe for exploration by forward-thinking nonprofits.

The impending wealth transfer from the Baby Boomer generation adds another layer of urgency to this scenario. As this generation enters retirement, we are witnessing the beginning of one of the largest wealth transfers in history, with estimates suggesting that around $84 trillion will change hands over the coming decades.[ii] A substantial portion of this wealth is expected to flow into charitable organizations, presenting an unprecedented opportunity for the nonprofit sector.

The implications of this wealth transfer are profound. Non-cash assets, often overlooked in traditional fundraising models, are now coming to the forefront. The transfer isn't just about the volume of wealth changing hands; it's about the forms that this wealth takes. For nonprofits, this means a shift in focus is needed. The days of primarily targeting cash donations are giving way to a more holistic approach, where non-cash assets become a key component of fundraising strategies.

By recognizing the potential of non-cash contributions, nonprofits can tap into a deeper well of resources, enabling them to expand their impact and reach. Moreover, we're finding that tax implications are having an outsized influence on what these donors with non-cash assets plan to do. Donors are looking for tax-efficient ways to support their favorite causes.

We also predict that midlevel and major giving will increase as a percentage of income for nonprofits in 2024, mostly due to a decline in general giving. Your nonprofit organization should prepare for an increase in major giving. So you may see an increase in non-cash gifts as major giving produces more of your fundraising revenue.

Leveraging the Trend of Non-Cash Giving

As the trend of non-cash giving gains momentum, nonprofits are presented with a unique opportunity to tap into this substantial resource. By encouraging non-cash contributions, organizations can significantly enhance their fundraising capabilities. To effectively capitalize on this trend, nonprofits need to employ strategic measures aimed at both existing donors and potential contributors. Here's how organizations can embrace and promote non-cash giving:

Educating Donors and Staff

Educating both donors and staff about non-cash giving is crucial. Launch comprehensive educational campaigns to inform donors about the benefits of non-cash giving, including potential tax advantages and the amplified impact of their contributions.

Kristin Hammett, Director of Nonprofit Success at The

Signatry, explained, "While the opportunity to expand giving capacity with noncash assets is significant, many donors aren't aware. A nonprofit leader or fundraiser can play a key role in facilitating generosity by educating donors. Sometimes all a leader needs to say is, 'Did you know you may be able to give more and pay less in tax if you give before the sale?'"

Simultaneously, equip your team with the necessary knowledge and skills to manage non-cash donations effectively, covering aspects such as valuation, legal implications, and processing. Educate your team about how donors can fulfill non-cash gifts using their Donor Advised Funds (DAFs).

Tailoring Strategies to Donor Profiles

Tailoring your strategies to align with the financial landscapes and preferences of different donor profiles is key. For younger donors or those in earlier stages of wealth accumulation, focus on assets that might be more prevalent in their portfolios, such as stocks or mutual funds. For older donors, especially those considering estate planning, emphasize how non-cash giving can play a pivotal role in their legacy planning, offering tax benefits and potentially reducing the taxable value of their estates.

In 2022, 61% of contributions to donor-advised funds (DAFs) at Schwab were non-cash assets.[iii] Donors took advantage of eliminating capital gain taxes by giving non-cash assets to their DAFs. Be sure to communicate about DAFs and how donors can contribute to your organization using this popular charitable giving vehicle.

Facilitating Non-Cash Contributions

Facilitating non-cash contributions is equally important. Ensure that the process of making non-cash donations is straightforward and supported. Consider establishing partnerships with financial institutions or platforms that can facilitate the transfer of various assets, making the donation process seamless and convenient for donors.

If the donor is giving complex assets such as real estate or shares in a business, it's vital to involve an expert like The Signatry (https://signatry.com) to help the donor maximize their donation.

Highlighting Non-Cash Giving Opportunities

Regularly highlighting the opportunities and impact of non-cash giving in your communications is vital. Feature stories and case studies that showcase the tangible difference non-cash contributions make. Create targeted campaigns during strategic times, such as the end of the fiscal year or during significant market events, to draw attention to the potential of non-cash giving.

Offering Recognition and Stewardship

Offering appropriate recognition and stewardship to donors who give non-cash assets is essential. Develop a comprehensive recognition program for your significant donors and include non-cash assets equal to cash gifts, and engage in ongoing stewardship activities. Kristin Hammett explained, "Donors who give non-cash assets are strategic, smart, or have advisors (and often all three!) These donors likely have capacity, regardless of the level they give at." Keep non-cash donors informed about the impact of their gifts and maintain a relationship that acknowledges their unique contributions to your organization's mission.

Consulting with Tax and Legal Professionals

Lastly, encourage donors to seek guidance from tax or financial advisors to understand the full scope of benefits and implications of their non-cash gifts. Ensure that your organization is also consulting with legal and financial experts to navigate the complexities of accepting, valuing, and acknowledging non-cash gifts properly.

"Nonprofits should know non-cash giving is complicated, but they don't need to be the expert," Kristin Hammett added. "They simply need to know there is an opportunity for expanded generosity and share that with the donor. When the donor expresses interest, the nonprofit can help connect the donor with an organization that specializes in this work. The Signatry, National Christian Foundation, or other Donor Advised Sponsors are good partners to work with donors and their advisors to assist in this generosity strategy."

By embracing these strategies, nonprofits can effectively leverage the trend of non-cash giving. This not only diversifies the organization's fundraising efforts but also aligns with the evolving preferences of donors, offering them a meaningful and tax-efficient way to contribute to the causes they care about. As we move further into 2024, the potential of non-cash giving is a frontier that all forward-thinking nonprofits should be prepared to explore.

Trend 2: Gen X and Millennial Importance

For years, the experts have talked about the importance of a strategy to reach Gen Z. Unfortunately, Gen X and Millennials are often overlooked, even though these are the generations that will provide a bulk of your nonprofit's support in the coming years.

Generation X, often referred to as the 'forgotten generation,' is anything but forgettable when it comes to philanthropy. These donors are at the peak of their careers and financial stability. Gen Xers are in a prime position to contribute significantly to causes they care about. A study found that Gen X donors give an average of $732 annually across four charities.[iv] Their pragmatic approach to giving, combined with a deep sense of social responsibility, makes them a key demographic for nonprofits.

Meanwhile, Millennials are coming into their own as influential donors, giving an annual average of $481,[v] driven by a desire to make a tangible impact on the world. Known for their tech-savviness, social consciousness, and preference for authentic, cause-driven narratives, Millennials are not just shaping the future of philanthropy; they are actively reshaping it with each passing day.

The importance of these generations extends beyond their financial contributions. Gen Xers and Millennials bring fresh perspectives, innovative ideas, and a strong preference for digital engagement, challenging nonprofits to evolve and adapt. At World Concern, we've had several donors in these generations who desire to volunteer in an impactful way that aligns with their professional capabilities. Their influence is also seen in the rising trends of social media fundraising, peer-to-peer giving, and a demand for transparency and measurable impact in their philanthropic endeavors.

While both Gen X and Millennials are pivotal in the philanthropic landscape of 2024, their giving behaviors exhibit distinct differences shaped by their unique life experiences and cultural influences.

Gen X, often characterized by their pragmatic approach, tend to be more strategic and reserved in their giving. They value discretion and are likely to be influenced by the practical outcomes and efficiency of their donations. This generation, having witnessed significant economic and technological changes, shows a preference for direct, impact-driven philanthropy.

Millennials, on the other hand, are driven by a deep sense of social responsibility and a desire for transparency. They are more inclined towards causes that align with their personal values. They tend to favor organizations that offer engagement and storytelling. Social media and peer influence play a significant role in their giving patterns, with a strong emphasis on shared experiences and community-based initiatives. Understanding these nuances is key for nonprofits aiming to engage with both generations in their fundraising efforts effectively.

Reaching Gen X and Millennial donors is not without challenges. Andrew Olsen, Sr. Vice President at DickersonBakker explained, "Unlike donors who belong to the Boomer or Greatest generations, these younger donors are less likely to say that they support a specific organization or nonprofit brand, instead preferring to align with a broader cause." Your organization will need to be transparent and show impact to close the loyalty gap with these generations.

How to Reach Gen X and Millennial Donors

Key to your efforts to grow the number of Gen X and Millennial donors is to understand that you'll use different channels to reach them. You'll also want to understand how donors in each of these two generations respond.

Embracing Digital and Social Media

To effectively engage Gen X and Millennials, nonprofits must recognize the centrality of digital platforms in their lives. Optimizing your online presence for user-friendliness and mobile responsiveness is crucial. A robust social media strategy utilizing platforms like Instagram, Twitter, and LinkedIn can significantly enhance engagement. These channels are perfect for sharing impactful stories, updates, and calls to action. Additionally, digital campaigns such as email marketing, peer-to-peer fundraising, and crowdfunding resonate well with these tech-savvy generations, offering them convenient ways to contribute and share.

Prioritizing Transparency and Demonstrating Impact

Both Gen X and Millennials value transparency and are keen to see the tangible impact of their donations. It's essential for nonprofits to communicate openly about how funds are being utilized. Regular updates, success stories, and detailed reports can help in showcasing the direct outcomes of their contributions. Engaging donors in the journey of their impact through volunteer opportunities or interactive platforms fosters a deeper connection with the cause.

Offering Flexible Engagement Opportunities

The desire for meaningful engagement beyond financial contributions is a hallmark of both Gen X and Millennials. They appreciate having a variety of ways to engage with a cause. Nonprofits can cater to this preference by offering diverse volunteering opportunities, advocacy initiatives, or educational events. Additionally, enabling supporters to fundraise on behalf of the organization taps into their networks and amplifies reach. Skills-based volunteering, in particular, can be a significant draw, allowing donors to contribute their professional expertise to the cause.

Personalizing Communication and Appeals

A personalized approach in communication is vital to resonate with Gen X and Millennials. Utilizing data to segment your audience and understand their preferences allows for more targeted and relevant messaging. Tailored communication that aligns with their values, aspirations, and motivations significantly increases engagement and support.

Fostering Community and a Sense of Shared Purpose

Creating a sense of community and shared purpose is particularly appealing to Gen X and Millennials. They are drawn to causes that provide a sense of belonging and collective impact. Establishing community spaces, either online or through in-person events, offers donors a platform to connect and share experiences. Emphasizing how each contribution is part of a larger movement reinforces the importance of every donation and strengthens the bond with the cause.

Organizations can build strong relationships with these crucial donor cohorts by employing these strategies, ensuring sustained support and a lasting impact on their missions. Andrew Olsen added, "The expectations that Gen X and Millennial donors have for the nonprofits they support will require organizations to change in significant ways over the next decade. Those who do make these changes stand to gain significant long-term support. Those who resist the need to change will likely be relegated to managing long-term revenue declines."

Trend 3: Emphasis on Donor Experience

A donor's experience encompasses much more than financial transactions. Donors desire engagement and connection with an organization. It's crucial to recognize the evolving expectations of donors, particularly their desire for involvement that goes beyond mere financial contributions.

This trend will expand on how nonprofits can create an enriching donor experience by focusing on relationship building, storytelling, skill-based volunteer opportunities, and demonstrating gratitude.

Beyond Financial Contributions: Cultivating Deeper Engagement

Donors increasingly seek a more active role in the causes they support. They want to see, feel, and know the impact of their contributions. Nonprofits can respond to this desire by offering various avenues for involvement. This could include inviting donors to participate in decision-making forums, providing them with regular updates on project progress, or even involving them in volunteer opportunities directly related to the organization's mission. At World Concern we have a Committee of committed supporters who meet regularly to here more about the work and get involved with initiatives like the Free Them 5k and Transform Gala. These supporters hear insider information about what we're working on and how their service or financial gifts are furthering the mission of the organization. By doing so, donors become partners in the cause, leading to a more fulfilling and engaging experience.

Skill-Based Volunteering: Leveraging Professional Expertise

Skill-based volunteering is a powerful way to deepen the donor experience. It allows individuals to contribute their professional expertise to a cause they are passionate about, going beyond monetary donations. Nonprofits can tap into this by identifying the specific skills and knowledge within their donor base and matching these with the organization's needs. This not only enhances the capacity of the nonprofit but also provides donors with a meaningful way to contribute, fostering a sense of personal investment and satisfaction in the success of the organization.

Emphasis on Relationship Building: The Core of Donor Experience

At the heart of an exceptional donor experience is relationship building. It's about understanding the individual behind the donation – their motivations, preferences, and how they wish to be involved with the organization. Personalized communication, recognizing and celebrating donor contributions, and providing opportunities for direct interaction with the beneficiaries of their donations are all strategies that can strengthen these relationships. Regular feedback loops, surveys, and donor appreciation events are also valuable in maintaining and nurturing these connections.

"We've known for a long time that the path to success with major donors is deep, authentic relationships," Andrew Olsen, Sr. Vice President at DickersonBakker elaborated. "We now see through donor surveys and individual donor interviews that younger donor cohorts have the exact same wants, desires, and expectations as older major donors, regardless of how much they are giving today. They want deeper connections to your cause. They want greater access to your senior leadership. They want clarity around your vision and your theory of change, they want to know exactly how their giving is creating transformational impact for those you serve, and they want to understand how partnering with you will enhance their own lives. Crafting experiences that deliver on these expectations will lead to increased donor retention and greater giving to your organization over time."

Incorporating these elements into the donor experience not only elevates the level of donor satisfaction but also fosters a community of dedicated supporters. It encourages a culture of philanthropy where donors are actively involved and invested in the organization's mission. As we progress through 2024, the emphasis on a holistic donor experience will be a defining factor in the success and sustainability of nonprofit organizations. This trend aims to equip you with the insights and strategies necessary to create a donor journey that is as rewarding for the donor as it is beneficial for your cause.

Enhancing Donor Experience

An exceptional donor experience can transform one-time givers into lifelong supporters. Here's how nonprofits can place a pronounced emphasis on the donor experience:

Understanding the Donor Journey

Start by mapping out the donor journey, from the initial awareness stage to the point of donation and beyond. Recognize that each interaction a donor has with your organization contributes to their overall experience. This includes every email, social media post, event invitation, and thank you letter. Aim for consistency, personalization, and a clear demonstration of value and impact at each touchpoint.

Personalization is Key

In an era where customization is the norm, personalizing the donor experience is non-negotiable. Use the data you have about your donors to tailor your communications and engagement strategies. Address donors by name, reference their past contributions, and make relevant suggestions based on their interests and giving history. Tools like CRM systems can automate this process, ensuring that each donor feels acknowledged and valued.

Foster Two-Way Communication

Engagement is a two-way street. Encourage and facilitate open communication with your donors. Provide them with platforms where they can voice their opinions, share their stories, or offer feedback. Regularly check in with surveys or polls to understand their perceptions and expectations. At World Concern, we've begun sending out monthly email surveys to a random group of 1,000 donors. We're getting ongoing feedback data over time to understand how donors feel and monitor any changes from month to month. By actively listening and responding, you show donors that their input is valued and that they play an integral role in your organization's journey.

At Food for the Hungry, we had a survey on the website at the end of the donation process. We asked questions about what the donor was interested in, including questions to determine the donor's interest in planned giving or church mobilization. This gave us great feedback and provided leads for our planned giving and church mobilization teams.

Deliver Impactful Reporting

Donors want to know that their contributions are making a difference. Provide clear, compelling reports on how their donations are being used and the impact they are creating. Use storytelling to bring these impacts to life, showcasing real stories of individuals or communities who have benefitted from their support. Visual aids like infographics or videos can make these reports more engaging and digestible.

Offer Exclusive Experiences

Create unique, memorable experiences for your donors. This could range from exclusive behind-the-scenes tours to special recognition events or even direct interactions with the beneficiaries of their donations.

Develop volunteer opportunities that are customized to the donor's experience and desire. At one organization I worked with, we had a program for volunteers to offer their time in a variety of fields of service. Those in the technology space would help architect solutions while volunteers in the medical field could take a trip to the field to work with doctors on the ground. When you personalize your volunteer opportunities, these individuals can become some of your most fervent supporters.

Such experiences not only enrich the donor's journey but also strengthen their emotional connection with your cause.

Acknowledge and Appreciate

Never underestimate the power of appreciation. Timely, heartfelt thank you messages, recognition in your organization's publications, or personalized tokens of appreciation can go a long way in making donors feel valued. I regularly give to nonprofit organizations to see how their donor welcome process works and get their ongoing donor communications. It amazes me how few organizations send simple "thank you" cards or letters after I give. This little gesture can create the most goodwill with a donor because so few people care enough to do it. Celebrate milestones, not just in terms of donations, but also the donor's journey and relationship with your organization.

Encourage Community and Belonging

Foster a sense of community among your donors. Involve them in peer networks, discussion forums, or special interest groups related to your cause. When donors feel part of a community, their engagement and loyalty to your organization increase.

By placing a strong emphasis on the donor experience, nonprofits can cultivate a base of passionate, dedicated supporters.

Trend 4: Hyper-Personalized Communications

When was the last time you were truly surprised by a nonprofit? For me, it was when I gave a gift to Medical Teams International. I received a standard email thank you and receipt. Next, I got a receipt in the mail. I received a long handwritten thank you card and a few days later, a phone call. Both the card and the phone call came from volunteers with the organization. These two tokens of appreciation were the personal touch that made it special and unique.

Hyper-personalized communications are ones where every message feels like it's crafted just for you. Imagine a world where every email, social media post, or newsletter you send out lands with the kind of precision and personal touch that makes each of your donors feel like they're the only one you're speaking to. What a great feeling! That's what hyper-personalization is all about, and it's not just a fancy trend; it's becoming a must-have in our noisy, bustling world.

"Conventional personalization doesn't involve understanding the supporter's preferences. It allows you to use their name, donation history, or location," John Walsh, Director of Annual Giving at St. Vladmir's Orthodox Theological Seminary, explained. "Not very reassuring for supporters. Whereas hyper-personalization takes into account each person's information and behaviors and speaks to their interests. You reach people when, where, and how they want to be reached."

In this trend, we'll peel back the curtain on how to make your communications truly stand out. It's all about getting to know your donors like never before – understanding what makes them tick, what they care about, and how they like to be involved. We're diving into the clever ways you can use data and technology not just to reach your audience, but to connect with them on a deeper level.

David Workman, Vice President at BBS & Associates (https://servantheart.com/), explained, "Most organizations barely scratch the surface of the kinds of personalized messaging you can deliver to your donors if you look at your data creatively."

We'll explore the magic of crafting messages that speak directly to each donor, making them feel seen and understood. And it's not about bombarding them with messages; it's about meaningful interactions, where each word is thoughtfully placed, each story is carefully told, and each message feels like a warm, personal conversation.

As we step through the pages of this trend, remember that at the heart of hyper-personalized communication is your story – the unique, compelling narrative of your nonprofit. By the end of this trend, you'll be ready to tell that story in a way that not only captures attention but also kindles a genuine, lasting connection with your donors. Let's dive in and turn every message into a moment of connection!

Hyper-personalized Communications and Your Donors

Leveraging this trend involves a blend of strategic insights, technological tools, and a dash of creativity. Let's explore the steps your organization can take to make the most of this transformative approach.

Collecting and Analyzing Data

John Walsh believes data is the first challenge you'll run into with hyper-personalization. "You will face different challenges when implementing hyper-personalization. The first of which has to do with data. You need to collect a vast amount of data, manage it, and ensure it is secure.

"To implement hyper-personalization, you need to collect quantitative and qualitative data. The more data you have the better the hyper-personalization. You can segment, automate, and hyper-personalize on every digital channel, including ads, websites, emails, push notifications, and even real-time support chat."

The journey to hyper-personalization begins with data. Start by gathering as much information as you can about your donors. This includes basic demographic details, past donation history, interaction records, and any other data points that can provide insights into their preferences and behavior. Use this data to segment your audience into different groups based on shared characteristics or interests.

Leveraging AI for Insights and Automation

This is where Artificial Intelligence (AI) comes into play. AI tools can sift through your data at incredible speeds, uncovering patterns and insights that might take humans much longer to identify. These insights allow you to predict donor behavior, understand what content resonates best with different segments, and determine the optimal times for sending communications.

AI can also automate many aspects of the communication process. From personalizing email subject lines to tailoring the content of newsletters based on individual preferences, AI makes it feasible to deliver a highly personalized experience to each donor without overwhelming your staff.

Crafting Tailored Content

Armed with insights from your data and AI analysis, you can now craft content that speaks directly to the interests and motivations of different donor segments. This could be stories that resonate with specific groups, updates on projects that align with their passions, or opportunities for involvement that match their preferences.

"Digital print technology takes this far beyond the mail merges of yesterday," David Workman shares. "Send your large donors a full color headline like, 'From <donor city> to Africa, your gift is saving lives!' Get your mail opened by saying, 'You've been carefully selected to represent citizens of <city, state> …' Reactivate more lapsed donors by reminding them, 'it's been <# of years> since we've had the privilege of your support.' You can create a wealth of meaningful messages with the data you already have."

For instance, if a segment of your donors is particularly interested in environmental projects, you can send them personalized updates about your organization's latest green initiatives, along with invitations to exclusive webinars or events related to environmental stewardship.

Continuous Learning and Iteration

Hyper-personalization is not a set-and-forget strategy. It requires continuous learning and iteration. Regularly analyze how your personalized communications are performing. Which messages are getting the most engagement? What content is driving donations? Use these insights to refine your approach continuously.

Feedback from your donors can also be invaluable. Consider sending out surveys or having informal chats to understand how your communications are being received and how you can improve.

By embracing the trend of hyper-personalized communications and leveraging tools like AI, your nonprofit can not only stand out in a crowded space but also build stronger, more meaningful relationships with your donors. It's about making every donor feel like they're your most important supporter, and in the process, turning them into passionate advocates for your cause.

Trend 5: Peer-to-Peer Fundraising

In 2024, peer-to-peer fundraising will continue to be a driving force for many nonprofit organizations. Unfortunately, we're not going to predict an increase in donor retention for peer-to-peer campaigns; instead, we're discussing a fresh, innovative approach to peer-to-peer fundraising. Imagine infusing the already powerful model of peer-to-peer fundraising with creative twists — gamified challenges that spark excitement, virtual events that draw crowds even from afar, and cause-linked merchandise collaborations that turn supporters into brand ambassadors.

Let's explore how these dynamic strategies are redefining peer-to-peer fundraising and setting new standards for donor engagement and campaign virality. The power of peer-to-peer fundraising lies in its ability to leverage personal networks, but when you add elements of gamification, influencer collaboration, and creative merchandise, you amplify its potential exponentially.

Nonprofits are revolutionizing peer-to-peer fundraising by embracing the power of gamification, turning traditional campaigns into captivating experiences that engage and motivate participants in a whole new way.

By integrating elements such as point scoring, competitions, and rewards into their campaigns, organizations are not only making the act of giving fun but are also tapping into the natural human love for challenges and recognition. This gamified approach fosters a spirited atmosphere that encourages friendly competition, increases participant engagement, and ultimately drives higher contributions.

The Leukemia & Lymphoma Society's Light The Night employs gamification in its peer-to-peer fundraising approach, enhancing the overall experience for participants. Individuals create their own fundraising pages and collaborate in teams, fostering a sense of community and collective effort. The campaign incorporates a leaderboard, which tracks the fundraising progress of both individuals and teams. This element introduces a layer of competition, naturally encouraging participants to engage more actively with their fundraising efforts. Recognition for top fundraisers and prizes serve as additional incentives, yet the primary focus remains on the collective goal of supporting the fight against leukemia and lymphoma. This method effectively combines the spirit of competition with the cause's communal ethos, making the fundraising process interactive and engaging.

Incorporating virtual events into peer-to-peer fundraising campaigns represents a strategic adaptation to the evolving landscape of donor engagement. These events offer a platform for participants to connect, share stories, and rally support for their causes, irrespective of geographical boundaries.

The virtual format not only broadens the potential participant pool but also provides a versatile and cost-effective medium for hosting a variety of events, from webinars and workshops to virtual walks or runs.

By leveraging technology, nonprofits can facilitate real-time interactions and foster a sense of community among participants, enhancing the collective fundraising experience. The data and insights gained from these virtual events also offer valuable feedback, allowing organizations to refine their strategies and better tailor future campaigns to their audience's preferences.

Cause-linked merchandise collaborations offer a creative and mutually beneficial avenue for nonprofits to raise funds and awareness. By partnering with brands to create specially designed products, nonprofits can tap into the brand's customer base while providing a tangible way for supporters to showcase their commitment to the cause. These collaborations often resonate deeply with consumers, as the purchase provides them with a physical item and the satisfaction of contributing to a meaningful cause.

For nonprofits, these partnerships extend beyond immediate fundraising; they serve as a powerful tool for brand exposure, helping to attract new supporters and reinforce relationships with existing ones. Carefully chosen collaborations that align with the nonprofit's values and mission can thus yield lasting benefits, turning everyday items into symbols of support and solidarity.

Peer-to-Peer Fundraising with a Twist

Peer-to-peer fundraising stands as a cornerstone of modern nonprofit strategies, and by infusing this approach with innovative elements such as gamification, virtual events, and cause-linked merchandise collaborations, nonprofits can significantly amplify their impact. Here's how organizations can leverage these dynamic strategies to breathe new life into their peer-to-peer campaigns.

Capitalizing on Gamification

Gamification injects a playful, competitive spirit into fundraising, making it an engaging experience for all involved. Nonprofits can introduce elements like point scoring, achievement badges, and leaderboards to track and showcase the efforts of participants. This motivates individuals and teams to increase their contributions and fosters a sense of accomplishment and recognition. To capitalize on this, organizations should:

- Design clear, achievable goals and milestones within their campaigns.
- Offer tangible rewards or recognition for top performers.
- Regularly update participants on their progress and standings to maintain engagement and momentum.

Maximizing Reach with Virtual Events

Virtual events break down geographical barriers, allowing nonprofits to engage with a global audience. These events can range from webinars and workshops to virtual galas or athletic challenges. The key to leveraging virtual events for peer-to-peer fundraising lies in:

- Ensuring high-quality, engaging content that resonates with the target audience.
- Using robust, user-friendly platforms that facilitate interaction and participation.
- Employing effective promotional strategies to maximize attendance and participation.

- Encouraging attendees to share their experiences on social media, further amplifying the campaign's reach.

Creating Impact with Cause-Linked Merchandise Collaborations

Merchandise collaborations provide a unique way for supporters to engage with and promote the cause. These partnerships, when executed thoughtfully, can significantly enhance brand visibility and create a sustained fundraising stream. To effectively leverage merchandise collaborations, nonprofits should:

- Partner with brands that share their values and resonate with their supporter base.
- Ensure that the merchandise is of high quality and has a clear connection to the cause.
- Develop a strategic marketing plan to promote the merchandise, highlighting the impact of each purchase.

- Engage supporters through storytelling, illustrating how the collaboration contributes to the organization's mission.

By integrating these innovative strategies into their peer-to-peer fundraising campaigns, nonprofits can create a more dynamic, engaging, and fruitful fundraising experience. Gamification, virtual events, and cause-linked merchandise collaborations not only attract and retain supporters but also foster a deeper connection between the community and the cause. As nonprofits navigate the ever-evolving landscape of fundraising, embracing these forward-thinking approaches will be key to staying relevant, engaging supporters, and driving meaningful change.

Trend 6: Reimagining Fundraising Events

The era of mundane, cookie-cutter galas is swiftly fading into the past, and perhaps, it's a change long overdue. Today's donors are more discerning than ever about how they choose to spend their time and resources. The traditional model of long, sales-pitch-heavy dinners is losing its allure. Instead, donors are craving something different, something more - they're seeking experiences.

"Unfortunately, non-profit fundraising events have a less-than-stellar reputation which oftentimes makes it difficult to get key donors and prospects to attend," explained Gary Heise, CEO of Premier Donor Strategies. "That model needs to change. Events must be presented with excellence. What is a better investment than treating your donors with an experience that reflects their significant value to your organization and its mission?"

In this trend, we acknowledge and address this pivotal shift in donor preferences. The appetite for passive participation is diminishing; donors no longer want to be mere spectators at these events. They are looking for engagement, interaction, and a sense of connection. They want to be part of something meaningful, to feel that they are contributing to a cause in a significant and experiential way.

We will explore how nonprofits can rise to meet these changing expectations, transforming their events into dynamic, immersive experiences that resonate deeply with attendees. From integrating technology and storytelling to fostering genuine interaction and community, this trend is a deep dive into redefining what a fundraising event can be. It's not just about changing the format or the venue; it's about rethinking the very essence of these gatherings, turning them from mere fundraisers into unforgettable experiences that inspire and mobilize.

"The most effective way to ignite the hearts of donors to give generously is by sharing inspirational stories of impact," Gary Heise added. "How is your ministry's work changing lives? Give real life examples. That's what will capture their attention at your event."

As we journey through this trend, let's embrace the opportunity to innovate, to create events that meet our donors' expectations and exceed them. The future of fundraising events is not just about raising funds; it's about building communities, creating memories, and igniting a shared passion for the cause.

How Should the Nonprofit Reimagine Fundraising Events?

You can transform your fundraising events into something that donors will want to attend and will motivate them to give. Your nonprofit must rethink your approach to fundraising events. It's no longer just about gathering a crowd and asking for donations; it's about creating an engaging, memorable experience that resonates with the audience's values and leaves a lasting impression. Here's how your nonprofit can reimagine fundraising events to align with the contemporary donor's expectations.

Creating Immersive Experiences

A common comment we heard from donors is the desire to have an invitation-worthy event. They desire an event they would be proud to bring friends or family to. Your goal: transform your events from standard gatherings into captivating experiences. One part of a successful formula for an immersive event is to incorporate interactive elements that engage attendees actively. For example, for our Transform major donor gala at World Concern, we brought in Adefua, a West African drumming group for a cultural experience. Attendees didn't just watch, they were invited to participate in a dance before the dinner began

Embrace technology to enrich these experiences further. Augmented and virtual reality can turn conventional settings into dynamic, immersive environments, offering attendees a unique and memorable encounter with your mission.

Focusing on Engagement

Another key to a successful gala in 2024 is to purposefully create engagement opportunities. Shift the spotlight from monologues to interactive dialogues. Replace long speeches with engaging activities that encourage active participation from your audience, forging a stronger emotional connection with your cause.

Gary Heise explained what donors want from today's events. "The value of getting major donors together and providing an impactful experience goes way beyond the money. Events are all about building relationships that result in deeper engagement and longer-term loyalty." Creating connection opportunities helps donors create meaningful interaction with fellow attendees, allowing them to network, share stories, and build a community united by a common purpose.

Personalizing the Attendee Experience

Tailor your event to resonate with the individual preferences of your donors using data and insights to add personal touches that make each attendee feel recognized and valued. At the World Concern Transform gala, donors are presented with live examples of the work. For example, we had a working water filter cleaning dirty water, an audio Bible station, and the Jesus Film playing in a scene made to look like a room in an African village. Offer choices within the event, such as selecting specific projects they wish to support or preferred activities. Personalization enhances the overall experience, making each donor's journey unique and memorable.

Visualizing Impact

Bring the results of your work to life by using compelling visuals, heartfelt testimonials, and live demonstrations to vividly showcase the difference your donors' contributions make. At this year's upcoming King's Schools auction & gala, we will have the high school drama team put on a short performance for attendees to see how their gift is making an impact. Incorporate real stories and interactive displays that allow attendees to see, feel, and understand the tangible impact of their support, deepening their commitment to your cause.

Integrating Modern Fundraising Tools

Embrace digital solutions to streamline and enhance the fundraising aspect of your events. Offer convenient options for ticket purchasing and donations through online platforms. Incorporate innovative tools like mobile giving, online auctions, or real-time fundraising trackers to engage a tech-savvy audience. Utilize social media to build anticipation, engage attendees during the event, and continue the conversation post-event, amplifying the reach and impact of your gathering.

Purposeful Follow-Up

Extend the event experience beyond the venue. Craft thoughtful follow-up communications that reflect the unique journey of each attendee. We send an automated email series after the King's Schools auction & gala and send personalized communications from the donor representatives to each attendee. It's crucial to share personalized thank you messages, memorable moments from the event, or updates on how contributions are being used. We also use a survey to seek feedback to continuously improve and show your donors that their opinions are valued and instrumental in shaping future events. We ask key attendees for one-on-one feedback of the event to get a feel for event perceptions.

"Time is the most valuable commodity for people in today's fast-paced culture. If your donors are giving you their precious time to attend an event, it better be well-planned, first-class, on-time and ultra-inspiring," Gary Heise told us. By reimagining your fundraising events with these strategies, your nonprofit can transcend traditional boundaries, offering an engaging, impactful, and unforgettable experience that resonates with donors and propels your mission forward.

Part 2: Tech-Powered Fundraising

Technology isn't a cure for bad fundraising tactics. Technology is an assistant to make the most of your best fundraising ideas.

In this section, we journey through trends 7 to 11, each focusing on a distinct aspect of tech-powered fundraising, from the integration of AI in fundraising tools to the innovative use of gamified strategies. Here's a preview of the invaluable insights and actionable strategies you'll uncover in these trends:

Trend 7: AI Integration in Fundraising Tools

In Trend 7, we explore the burgeoning role of Artificial Intelligence in revolutionizing fundraising efforts. AI's capacity to analyze data, predict trends, and personalize donor interactions is changing the game. This trend not only demystifies AI but also provides a roadmap for integrating these advanced technologies into your fundraising strategies. You'll learn about AI-powered analytics that can predict donor behavior, tools that automate donor communications, and systems that streamline operations, freeing up valuable resources for mission-driven activities.

Trend 8: Investment in Owned Media

Trend 8 emphasizes the importance of investing in owned media — a critical component in today's fragmented digital landscape. As traditional advertising becomes more challenging and less effective, developing a robust owned media strategy — including blogs, newsletters, and other content platforms — becomes crucial. This trend guides you through creating compelling content that resonates with your audience, employing SEO best practices to enhance visibility, and leveraging analytics to refine your approach. You'll discover how to build a loyal community around your content, turning passive readers into active supporters.

Trend 9: Growing Significance of Marketing Automation

In Trend 9, we explore the world of marketing automation and its growing significance in nonprofit fundraising. With the increasing complexity and scale of digital interactions, automation tools are no longer a luxury but a necessity. This trend explores how automating repetitive tasks can free up time for your team to focus on strategic, high-impact activities. You'll learn about setting up automated email campaigns, social media posting, and donor segmentation strategies designed to increase your communications' efficiency and effectiveness.

Trend 10: TikTok's Launch of a Charity Tool

Trend 10 focuses on the predicted launch of TikTok's charity tool and its implications for nonprofit fundraising. As one of the fastest-growing social media platforms, TikTok offers immense potential for reaching and engaging younger audiences. If TikTok follows their TikTok Shops with a TikTok giving tool, you'll want to be prepared for it. You'll gain insights into crafting a TikTok strategy that aligns with your organization's goals and resonates with the platform's dynamic, content-hungry audience.

Trend 11: Use of Interactive and Gamified Fundraising

Finally, Trend 11 brings you to the cutting edge of fundraising with interactive and gamified strategies. As donor expectations evolve, the demand for engaging, experiential interactions is on the rise. This trend provides a comprehensive overview of incorporating game mechanics into your fundraising campaigns to boost engagement and contributions. You'll explore the psychology behind gamification, learn how to design challenges and rewards that motivate participation, and discover tools that can help you create immersive, game-like experiences for your donors.

Throughout Part 2, you'll find a common thread: the power of technology to transform the way nonprofits connect with donors, streamline operations, and maximize impact. Each trend not only highlights the latest trends but also provides practical advice on implementing these technologies in your own fundraising efforts. Whether you're a tech enthusiast eager to explore the latest innovations or a fundraising professional looking to enhance your strategies with tech-driven solutions, this section offers a wealth of guidance.

Trend 7: AI Integration in Fundraising Tools

While generative AI has been capturing much of the press's attention, its application within the realm of nonprofit fundraising extends far beyond. From sophisticated AI tools that fine-tune donor segmentations to advanced analytics platforms that dissect and interpret data, AI is revolutionizing the way nonprofits operate, communicate, and fundraise.

In this trend, we'll unpack the role of AI in the nonprofit world. While generative AI opens up new avenues for content creation and donor engagement, it's just the tip of the iceberg. We'll explore how AI can empower your organization to make smarter decisions, identify key donor segments, predict giving patterns, and personalize outreach on an unprecedented scale. This isn't about replacing the human touch; it's about augmenting your capabilities and freeing your team to focus on what they do best – nurturing relationships and driving your mission forward.

The smart nonprofit in 2024 is not just a passive observer but an active experimenter. It's about being agile, embracing new technologies, and discovering how different AI tools can be woven into the fabric of your fundraising strategies to yield remarkable results.

"If you've ever attempted repairs on your home or car, you know the right tool can make all the difference," explained David Workman, Vice President at BBS & Associates. "But you'll never know if there's a tool you can use to make a project more efficient, or produce a better result, unless you crack open the toolbox and rummage around. Make this the year you get your hands dirty in the AI toolbox — you might be surprised at what you find."

Whether you're taking your first steps into the world of AI or looking to enhance your existing toolkit, this trend is your compass in the ever-evolving landscape of AI-driven fundraising.

By the end of this exploration, you'll have a clear understanding of the potential of AI and how it can be harnessed to transform your organization's approach to fundraising. It's not all pretty. There are countless tools right now that just aren't effective. But the technology is advancing at an unbelievable pace, and by the end of 2024, we'll look back and acknowledge AI has had a transformative effect on many nonprofits.

AI Fundraising Tools

Technology is rapidly advancing, and nonprofits are uniquely positioned to harness the power of Artificial Intelligence to revolutionize their fundraising strategies. Here's how your organization can take advantage of the diverse AI offerings to maximize fundraising in 2024:

Donor Segmentation and Personalization

AI excels at parsing through vast amounts of data and identifying patterns that humans might miss. By leveraging AI for donor segmentation, your organization can categorize donors based on their behavior, preferences, and giving history. This segmentation allows for highly personalized communication strategies. Tailored messages resonate more deeply with donors, making them feel seen and understood, and significantly increasing the chances of engagement and donations.

AI is also making a mark on prospect identification and research. Entrenched companies like DonorSearch have embraced AI in their tools, making them even more effective at identifying potential midlevel and major donors.

Predictive Analytics

Predictive analytics is another area where AI can significantly benefit your nonprofit. AI algorithms can predict future giving patterns based on historical data, helping you understand when donors are most likely to give and what amount they are likely to contribute. This information enables you to time your campaigns more effectively and tailor your asks to fit the donor's giving potential, thereby maximizing the chances of fundraising success.

Automating Routine Tasks

AI can automate various routine tasks, freeing up your team to focus on more strategic activities. From sending out personalized thank you emails to managing donation records, AI can handle a multitude of administrative tasks efficiently and error-free. This not only increases operational efficiency but also ensures that your staff can devote more time to building relationships with donors and driving your mission forward.

Engaging Donors with AI-Generated Content

While generative AI has been in the spotlight, its application in creating engaging content for donors is undeniably powerful. From drafting personalized fundraising letters to creating compelling narratives for your campaigns, AI can assist in generating content that appeals to your donors. This ensures a consistent and appealing communication strategy and helps maintain a steady engagement with your donors.

Enhancing Donor Experience with Chatbots

AI-powered chatbots can significantly enhance the donor experience by providing immediate responses to queries, guiding donors through the donation process, and offering personalized recommendations based on the donor's interaction history. This 24/7 availability and personalized interaction make donors feel supported and valued, contributing to a positive experience and fostering long-term relationships.

Ethical Considerations and Transparency

As you integrate AI into your fundraising strategies, it's crucial to navigate the ethical considerations and maintain transparency with your donors. Be clear about how you're using AI and the data it's analyzing. Ensure that you're upholding the highest standards of data privacy and security. By being transparent and ethical in your use of AI, you build trust with your donors, which is fundamental to any successful fundraising strategy.

Implementing AI in Your Nonprofit

To effectively implement AI in your nonprofit, start with a clear strategy. Identify the areas where AI can have the most significant impact, whether it's donor communication, data analysis, or operational efficiency. Invest in the right tools and platforms that align with your organization's needs and capacity. And perhaps most importantly, ensure that your team is trained and comfortable with these new technologies.

Trend 8: Investment in Owned Media

Organic social reach is dead. Social networks and social marketing is different today than it was even a year ago. The days of relying solely on organic reach on platforms like Facebook, Instagram, or Twitter are behind us. The digital landscape is changing, and the once-reliable organic reach on social networks is now a challenge, with platforms constantly tweaking their algorithms, making it harder for nonprofit messages to be seen without significant investment.

In 2024, the answer lies in a strategic pivot towards content creation and content marketing – a move towards owned media. Let's explore how investing in owned media not only circumvents the limitations of organic reach on social networks but also establishes a direct, unmediated connection with your audience.

This situation underscores the importance of investing

in owned content. By developing blogs, newsletters, and other digital content, nonprofits create a stable and controlled space to convey their stories, missions, and calls to action, free from the unpredictability of social media algorithms and the crowded, competitive nature of these platforms.

Owned content is more than just a communication tool; it's a strategic asset for nonprofits. It ensures a direct, unfiltered line of communication with the audience, fostering deeper and more meaningful engagement. When nonprofits control their content, they have complete command over their narrative, how it's presented, and the experience it offers the audience. This autonomy allows organizations to create messages that resonate deeply with their supporters' values and interests. Moreover, a strong content strategy doesn't just draw new supporters; it nurtures loyalty among the existing base, transforming casual readers into committed advocates.

"Creating content is often looked at as a 'naughty phrase' inside of our nonprofit hallways because it has a reputation of costing a lot, fundraising a little, and distracting the teams that should be doing the 'other important tasks' of communicating about our cause," explained Casey Helmick, President of Terra Firma Audio. "And the truth is - those criticisms are often accurate! But for those nonprofits that can create vital content that your supporters rely on and look forward to, the sky is the limit. The ability to create a deeper relationship, through vital content, with your supporters has become the lifeblood of the modern nonprofit organization."

By building a robust content repository, nonprofits can establish their authority, demonstrate their impact, and cultivate trust, all of which are crucial in an environment where credibility and authenticity are invaluable.

How to Invest in More Owned Media

Before diving into content creation, it's essential for nonprofits to craft a strategic content plan. This plan should align with the organization's overall goals, mission, and the interests of its target audience. Start by defining your key messages, identifying the topics that will resonate with your audience, and setting clear objectives for what you want your content to achieve. Whether it's raising awareness, driving donations, or recruiting volunteers, your content should have a purpose that ties back to your organizational goals.

Creating High-Quality, Relevant Content

The heart of your owned media strategy lies in the creation of high-quality, relevant content. This content should not only inform but also inspire and engage your audience.

"When developing content, ask yourself, 'is this something I'd read or watch? Is this something I'd find interesting?' If not, your audiences probably won't either," explained nonprofit branding expert Chad DeMiguel. "Be relentless with your team in ensuring your content is providing real value to your donors - whether it's informative, inspiring or entertaining. There's too much noise in the world. Make sure you're giving them something worth paying attention to."

Invest time in understanding what your audience cares about and how your organization's work aligns with those interests. Use storytelling to share success stories, case studies, or beneficiary testimonials that bring your mission to life. Remember, content can take many forms – from blog posts and articles to videos, podcasts, and infographics. Diversify your content formats to cater to different preferences and increase engagement.

Optimizing for Search Engines

To ensure that your content reaches the widest possible audience, it's crucial to optimize it for search engines. This practice, known as Search Engine Optimization (SEO), involves using targeted keywords, crafting compelling meta descriptions, and structuring your content in a way that's favored by search engine algorithms. SEO helps improve the visibility of your content in search engine results, driving organic traffic to your website and increasing the chances of engagement and conversion.

Promoting Content Across Channels

Creating great content is just the beginning. To maximize its impact, promote your content across multiple channels. This includes your organization's website, email newsletters, and social media platforms. Sharing your content across different channels not only increases its reach but also provides multiple touchpoints for your audience to engage with your organization. Additionally, consider leveraging partnerships or collaborations with other organizations, influencers, or media outlets to further amplify your content's reach.

Measuring and Adapting

Finally, it's vital to measure the performance of your content and use those insights to refine your strategy. Track key metrics such as page views, engagement rates, and conversion rates to understand how your content is performing. Pay attention to audience feedback and be prepared to adapt your content strategy based on what's resonating with your audience. Continuously refining your approach will ensure that your owned media strategy remains effective and aligned with your organization's evolving goals and the changing interests of your audience.

Investing in owned media is a powerful way for nonprofits to build a direct, lasting connection with their audience. By developing a strategic content plan, creating high-quality content, optimizing for search engines, promoting across channels, and continuously measuring and adapting, nonprofits can effectively leverage their owned media to advance their mission and achieve their fundraising goals.

Trend 9: Growing Significance of Marketing Automation

In 2024, we will need to do more with less. Few organizations are going to be on a hiring spree, so how do we get the most out of our marketing and fundraising efforts?

Marketing automation.

In this environment, the ability to efficiently manage campaigns, personalize interactions, and maximize donor engagement is not just beneficial – it's essential. Marketing automation stands out as a key tool, providing a range of solutions to streamline operations, tailor communications, and analyze campaign results effectively.

Marketing automation refers to the use of software and technology to automate, streamline, and measure marketing tasks and workflows, increasing operational efficiency and growing revenue faster. In the context of nonprofits, marketing automation becomes a powerful tool, not just for saving time and resources, but also for fostering deeper, more meaningful relationships with donors, volunteers, and supporters.

Nonprofits typically use marketing automation to handle repetitive tasks such as email marketing, social media posting, and other website actions. The technology enables organizations to send out automated, yet personalized, messages to different segments of their audience. This level of personalization is critical in a landscape where donors expect communications to be tailored to their interests, giving history, and engagement with the organization.

Beyond sending out mass emails, marketing automation tools can track the engagement of recipients, allowing nonprofits to see who opened an email, clicked on links, or took specific actions. This data is invaluable. It provides insights into donor behavior, helping nonprofits refine their messaging, segment their audience more effectively, and send targeted communications that are likely to resonate and elicit a response.

Marketing automation can play a pivotal role in donor retention and engagement strategies. It can automate the process of sending out thank you emails, birthday wishes, or anniversary messages acknowledging the duration of a donor's support. These gestures, though automated, can feel personal and genuine, helping to strengthen the relationship between the donor and the organization.

For fundraising, marketing automation can be used to create and manage campaigns more efficiently. For instance, a nonprofit can set up a drip email campaign for a fundraising event, automating the process of sending out reminders, updates, and thank you messages. This not only ensures consistent communication but also frees up staff to focus on other crucial aspects of the event.

Marketing automation is a multifaceted tool that, when used effectively, can transform the marketing efforts of a nonprofit. It allows for more personalized, efficient, and strategic communication, ensuring that the right message reaches the right person at the right time. As nonprofits continue to navigate the digital landscape, the role of marketing automation is set to become more integral, driving engagement, supporting fundraising efforts, and ultimately, helping organizations to fulfill their mission more effectively.

How Does Your Nonprofit Use Marketing Automation?

Nonprofits can harness the power of marketing automation in various ways to streamline their operations, enhance donor engagement, and ultimately, drive their fundraising efforts. By implementing marketing automation effectively, nonprofits can not only save time but also create more impactful, personalized communication strategies.

Automating Routine Communications

One of the primary uses of marketing automation in nonprofits is to automate routine communications. This includes sending out welcome emails to new subscribers, thank you messages to donors, and regular newsletters to keep the community informed and engaged. By automating these communications, nonprofits ensure that no interaction is overlooked and that every supporter feels acknowledged and valued. Furthermore, automation allows for personalization at scale, enabling organizations to tailor messages based on the recipient's past interactions, preferences, and engagement level.

Segmenting Audiences for Targeted Campaigns

Marketing automation tools provide robust features for audience segmentation. Nonprofits can categorize their supporters based on various criteria, such as donation history, event participation, or engagement with past campaigns. By segmenting their audience, organizations can create more targeted and relevant campaigns. For instance, a nonprofit can send different versions of a fundraising appeal to recurring donors, one-time donors, and prospects, each version tailored to the specific group's history and relationship with the organization.

Tracking Donor Engagement and Behavior

Marketing automation platforms offer analytics and tracking capabilities that allow nonprofits to monitor the performance of their campaigns and understand donor behavior. Organizations can track metrics such as open rates, click-through rates, and conversion rates to gauge the effectiveness of their emails and other marketing efforts. This data is invaluable for optimizing campaigns, understanding what resonates with the audience, and refining future communications to maximize engagement and donations.

Nurturing Donor Relationships

Nonprofits can use marketing automation to nurture their relationships with donors over time. By setting up automated email sequences, organizations can keep donors informed about how their contributions are being used, share success stories, and offer opportunities for further involvement. This consistent, thoughtful communication helps to build trust, foster loyalty, and encourage recurring donations.

Streamlining Event Management

Marketing automation can significantly streamline the management of events, a crucial aspect of fundraising for many nonprofits. From sending out invitations and registration links to following up with attendees post-event, automation ensures that every step of the event is executed smoothly and efficiently. It also enables organizations to send targeted communications based on attendees' interactions during the event, enhancing the overall experience and deepening their engagement with the cause.

Marketing automation offers a multitude of benefits for nonprofits, from automating routine tasks and personalizing communications to tracking engagement and streamlining event management. By leveraging these tools effectively, organizations can not only enhance their operational efficiency but also create deeper, more meaningful connections with their supporters. As the digital landscape continues to evolve, the strategic use of marketing automation will be increasingly critical for nonprofits looking to maximize their impact and advance their mission.

Trend 10: Prediction: TikTok Launches Charity Marketplace

Here's a prediction: TikTok launches a charity marketplace similar to the recently launched TikTok shops. The form will be a platform where charities can effectively showcase their initiatives and directly engage with a vast audience to garner support and donations.

Known for its engaging content and extensive, diverse user base, TikTok's predicted creation of a charitable giving marketplace is expected to revolutionize the way nonprofits interact with the younger demographic. The platform's strength in short-form video content can become a powerful tool for charities, enabling them to convey their stories, share their impact, and inspire action in a compelling, visually captivating manner.

TikTok currently offers fundraising tools[vi] for

nonprofits, including a Cause Link for your profiles and Donation Stickers for videos and livestream. These features are handy, but a charity marketplace would be a transformational opportunity for nonprofits.

A TikTok giving platform could usher in a new era of social media-driven philanthropy, where the power of virality is harnessed for social good. As content on TikTok often trends based on creativity, emotional appeal, and relatability, nonprofits have the opportunity to craft campaigns that not only raise funds but also raise awareness on a large scale.

The platform's algorithm, which promotes content based on user interaction rather than follower count, levels the playing field for all organizations, allowing smaller nonprofits to gain visibility alongside larger ones. This democratization of content sharing means that with the right message and creative approach, any nonprofit can engage a vast audience, turning viewers into advocates and donors, and driving real-world impact through the power of social media.

Perhaps it's not TikTok but X or Snapchat that transforms social giving. Whatever the platform, nonprofits should be prepared for platform innovation.

How to Prepare for a Social Media Giving Platform

As social media platforms continue to evolve and introduce new ways for users to engage and contribute, nonprofits must remain agile and proactive in their approach. Preparing for platforms like TikTok or others to introduce new giving features involves strategic planning, understanding the platform's unique dynamics, and crafting content that resonates with the audience. Here are several steps nonprofits can take to ensure they are ready for these new opportunities:

Understand the Platform's User Base and Content Style

Nonprofits should start by deeply understanding the platform's user base and the type of content that performs well. TikTok, for instance, is popular among younger audiences who appreciate creativity, authenticity, and a touch of humor. Familiarizing yourself with trending formats, challenges, and hashtags can provide valuable insights into crafting content that aligns with user preferences and the platform's unique style.

Build and Train a Dedicated Social Media Team

Given the fast-paced nature of platforms like TikTok, having a dedicated social media team is crucial. This team should be equipped to create, monitor, and engage with content regularly. Training the team on best practices for the platform, understanding analytics, and staying up-to-date with the latest trends and algorithm changes can ensure your nonprofit remains relevant and engaged with its audience.

Develop a Robust Content Strategy

Content is king on social media platforms, and having a robust content strategy is essential. Your strategy should include a mix of storytelling, showcasing the impact of donations, and interactive content that encourages user participation. The content should be authentic and align with your nonprofit's mission and values, while also being tailored to the platform's format and user preferences.

Engage and Collaborate with Influencers

Collaborating with influencers who align with your nonprofit's values can significantly amplify your reach and impact. Influencers can help bring credibility, expand your audience, and drive engagement and donations. Identify and build relationships with influencers who are passionate about your cause and have a genuine connection with their followers.

Integrate Giving Features Seamlessly

When platforms introduce giving features, it's crucial to integrate them seamlessly into your content and engagement strategy. Make the process of donating as easy and intuitive as possible. Clearly communicate how users can contribute through the platform and the impact their donation will make. Regularly recognize and thank your donors, fostering a community of engaged and recurring supporters.

Monitor, Analyze, and Adapt

Lastly, continuously monitor the performance of your content and fundraising campaigns. Platforms like TikTok provide analytics that can offer insights into user engagement, content reach, and more. Use this data to understand what works and what doesn't, and be prepared to adapt your strategy accordingly. Being responsive to analytics and user feedback will ensure your nonprofit stays ahead of the curve and maximizes its fundraising potential on the platform.

By taking these steps, nonprofits can be well-prepared to leverage new giving features on platforms like TikTok. Embracing these opportunities requires a blend of strategic planning, content creativity, and community engagement – all aimed at connecting with users in meaningful ways and driving social impact through digital channels.

Trend 11: Use of Interactive and Gamified Fundraising

A nonprofit will develop an interactive and gamified fundraising method in 2024 that motivates tens of thousands of new donors to support their work.

As organizations continually seek innovative ways to engage donors and amplify their fundraising efforts, the integration of gamification into giving strategies is poised to take center stage. This prediction is grounded in the evolving donor landscape, where the desire for interactive, engaging, and rewarding experiences is becoming increasingly pronounced.

We envision a scenario where a nonprofit organization successfully pioneers a gamified giving campaign, setting a new standard for donor engagement. This campaign would seamlessly blend the elements of gaming – such as point scoring, achievements, and competitive leaderboards – with the altruistic act of giving. The result is a dynamic and immersive experience that not only captivates donors but also fosters a deeper connection to the cause.

The success of such a gamified system hinges on its ability to transform the traditional donation process into an interactive journey. Donors would not just be contributing financially; they would be actively participating in a narrative where every contribution propels them forward, unlocks new levels of impact, and offers tangible rewards and recognition. This approach effectively leverages the innate human love for challenges and achievements, channeling it towards philanthropic goals.

In 2024, we predict that this pioneering approach by a nonprofit will set a precedent, demonstrating the immense potential of gamified giving systems. This campaign will not only achieve its fundraising objectives but also ignite a trend within the sector, inspiring other organizations to explore and adopt gamification in their fundraising strategies.

How to Create Your Own Gamified Fundraising Strategy

Creating a gamified giving system begins with laying a solid foundation. Nonprofits should start by defining clear goals for the campaign, such as increasing donor engagement, raising a certain amount of funds, or attracting new donors. Understanding the target audience is crucial – knowing their preferences, behaviors, and motivations will inform the design of the gamification elements. Once the groundwork is laid, the organization can start building the structure of the gamified system, determining the rules of the game, the points system, and the rewards for different levels of participation.

Incorporating Engaging Gamification Elements

The heart of a gamified giving system lies in its ability to engage and motivate donors. Incorporating elements like points, badges, leaderboards, and challenges can transform the giving experience. For instance, donors could earn points for every dollar donated or for sharing the campaign on social media. Achieving certain points could unlock badges or titles, and a leaderboard could display top contributors, fostering a sense of competition and community. Challenges or missions related to the nonprofit's cause can further engage donors, especially if completing them leads to tangible impacts, like funding a specific project or reaching a community goal.

Leveraging Technology for Seamless Integration

Technology plays a pivotal role in executing a gamified giving system effectively. Choosing the right platform is essential – it should support the gamification elements, be user-friendly, and ensure a seamless donation process. Integration with the nonprofit's website and social media is also crucial for maintaining a cohesive presence and making it easy for donors to participate and share their contributions. Additionally, the system should be equipped with analytics tools to track engagement, monitor progress, and gather insights for future campaigns.

Creating a Rewarding Donor Experience

The success of a gamified giving campaign largely depends on the donor experience. Nonprofits should ensure that the system not only incentivizes participation but also makes donors feel valued and appreciated. Tailoring rewards to align with donors' interests can increase motivation – these could be tangible items, exclusive experiences, or public recognition. Regular updates on the campaign's progress and the impact of donations reinforce the value of each contribution and foster a sense of shared achievement.

Promoting and Sustaining Engagement

Promotion is key to the success of a gamified giving campaign. Utilizing various channels – from email marketing to social media – can help reach a wider audience and attract participants. Engaging storytelling, compelling visuals, and clear calls-to-action are crucial for capturing attention and driving participation. Once the campaign is underway, maintaining momentum is essential. Regular communication, celebrating milestones, and showcasing the impact of collective efforts keep donors engaged and motivated to reach the campaign goals.

In conclusion, creating a gamified giving system or campaign offers nonprofits a dynamic way to engage donors, raise funds, and promote their cause. By thoughtfully designing the framework, incorporating engaging elements, leveraging technology, creating a rewarding experience, and actively promoting the campaign, organizations can transform traditional giving into an interactive, enjoyable, and impactful journey.

Part 3: Community & Collaboration

In this increasingly interconnected world, the power of collective effort and shared goals cannot be overstated. This section explores how nonprofits can leverage partnerships, harness the influence of social media, and embrace innovative donation models to foster a sense of community and drive collaborative success. Trends 12 through 15 provide a roadmap for building stronger, more impactful relationships between nonprofits, their supporters, and broader networks.

Trend 12: Global Collaboration and Fundraising

In Trend 12, we examine the expanding scope of global collaboration and its profound impact on fundraising. As geographical boundaries become less relevant, nonprofits have the opportunity to engage with a global audience and collaborate with international partners. This trend explores strategies for building global networks, sharing resources, and leveraging cross-border partnerships to amplify impact and reach fundraising goals.

Trend 13: Cause-Related Marketing Partnerships

Trend 13 focuses on the power of cause-related marketing partnerships. These collaborations between nonprofits and businesses can significantly boost fundraising efforts while providing mutual benefits. We'll discuss how to forge meaningful partnerships, align your missions and values, and create campaigns that resonate with consumers, driving both awareness and contributions.

Trend 14: Rise of Social Media Influencers in Fundraising

In Trend 14, we look at the influential world of social media influencers and their role in reshaping fundraising. Influencers can act as powerful advocates for your cause, leveraging their platforms to increase visibility, credibility, and support. This trend offers insights into selecting the right influencers, building authentic relationships, and crafting campaigns that harness their reach and resonance to inspire action and donations.

Trend 15: Adoption of Subscription Model Donations

Trend 15 explores the emerging trend of subscription model donations, a concept that offers a steady and predictable revenue stream for nonprofits while providing donors with a convenient and consistent way to support their favorite causes. We'll discuss the benefits of this model, how to implement and manage subscription-based giving programs, and strategies for maintaining and growing your subscriber base.

Part 3 of this book emphasizes the importance of community and collaboration in the ever-evolving landscape of nonprofit fundraising. Through global partnerships, cause-related marketing, influencer engagement, and innovative donation models, nonprofits can create a network of support that extends far beyond individual contributions, driving collective impact and lasting change.

Trend 12: Global Collaboration and Fundraising

In 2024, corporations, governments, foundations, and nonprofits will work together to fight global poverty.

This year is anticipated to mark a significant shift towards a more united approach in addressing social challenges. The trend explores how nonprofits, corporations, foundations, and governments are increasingly joining forces, moving away from working in silos to a more integrated, problem-solving partnership.

The shift is partly driven by the changing expectations of the younger generation. They are calling for corporations to engage beyond just financial contributions, urging them to play a more active role in creating and implementing sustainable solutions. As a result, 2024 is expected to see corporations transition from being mere donors to becoming involved partners in social initiatives.

This trend delves into the mechanics of this collaboration. It highlights the importance of aligning goals, sharing resources, and maintaining transparent operations as the pillars of successful partnerships. We also discuss how technology is playing a crucial role in enabling these collaborations, making it easier to communicate, scale efforts, and measure the impact of these collective actions.

This represents a significant change from working in isolation to adopting a comprehensive strategy. It acknowledges that tackling global poverty's intricate challenges demands the collective effort, resources, and know-how of various sectors. By joining forces, the effectiveness of each contribution is magnified, resulting in solutions that are not only more enduring but also have a broader reach.

The Texas state government has been at the leading edge of public-private partnerships. For example, the Texas Department of Family Services partners with CarePortal, a network of churches, to help children and families at a local level. This partnership has helped 16,000 children.[vii]

Collaboration reflects a growing understanding that tackling major social issues is a shared responsibility, transcending the boundaries of any single organization or sector. The trend also signifies an alignment with the values of a new generation of consumers and donors who seek active, meaningful engagement from corporations in social causes. Ultimately, this movement towards collaborative action not only holds the promise of making a more significant dent in global poverty but also sets a precedent for addressing other pressing global challenges in a more integrated and effective manner.

How Does Your Nonprofit Adapt to This Trend?

Nonprofits must recognize collaboration not just as a beneficial approach, but as a core strategy in their efforts to combat global poverty. Embracing collaboration means actively seeking partnerships with corporations, governments, and other nonprofits that share a common goal. It involves being open to sharing resources, expertise, and insights to create synergies that amplify impact. Nonprofits should foster a culture that values collective over individual success, focusing on the broader objective of alleviating poverty.

Building Strong, Transparent Partnerships

Creating and maintaining strong partnerships is crucial in this collaborative environment. Nonprofits should prioritize transparency and open communication, establishing clear terms and expectations from the outset. Regular meetings and updates can help keep all parties aligned on goals, strategies, and progress. Establishing trust through consistent, reliable actions and demonstrating a commitment to the shared mission is also important. Recognizing and respecting each partner's contributions and expertise is vital for a fruitful collaboration.

Leveraging Technology for Effective Collaboration

Technology can be a powerful enabler of collaboration, helping partners coordinate efforts, share data, and measure impact more effectively. Nonprofits should invest in platforms and tools that facilitate seamless communication and information sharing among partners.

"My organization uses an excellent data analytics tool that allows me to gather, track, and monitor the progress on actionable items that have a quick turnaround time," Andrea Danz explained. "I appreciate having this software because it saves me time when I need to make quick decisions and provides extensive data to help me and those partners I work with to mitigate risks. Having access to such valuable technology makes my job that much easier."

Using project management software, shared databases, and collaborative platforms can help keep everyone on the same page and streamline joint efforts. Additionally, data analytics tools can provide insights that drive more informed decision-making and help partners track and assess the impact of their collaborative initiatives.

Adapting to a Changing Donor Landscape

As the trend towards collaboration aligns with the

values of a new generation of donors, nonprofits must adapt their messaging and engagement strategies accordingly. This involves communicating not just the outcomes of their initiatives but also highlighting the collaborative nature of their efforts. Showcasing how partnerships are contributing to the broader goal of alleviating global poverty can resonate with donors who value collective action and social responsibility. Nonprofits should leverage stories of successful collaborations to inspire and engage their supporters, demonstrating that their contributions are part of a larger, concerted effort to effect change.

Dealing with the trend towards collaboration in combating global poverty requires nonprofits to embrace a mindset of unity, build strong and transparent partnerships, leverage technology effectively, and adapt to the evolving expectations of donors. By doing so, they can enhance their impact, drive sustainable solutions, and play a pivotal role in this collective journey towards a poverty-free world.

Trend 13: Cause-Related Marketing Partnerships

Businesses want to support causes that align with their customers and staff. In 2024, this will continue to grow with businesses using their marketing budget to demonstrate how much they care about specific causes.

This trend is about how nonprofits can team up with businesses to boost their fundraising, spread their message, and make a bigger impact. Nowadays, more companies want to support important causes, and that's great news for nonprofits. These partnerships can bring extra resources, help reach new people, and create powerful campaigns that people really care about.

We'll guide you through setting up successful partnerships with businesses. We'll talk about how to find the right company to partner with and how to create campaigns that truly reflect your nonprofit's goals while also fitting well with the company's brand. We'll also dive into how to keep these partnerships strong and beneficial for everyone involved. By understanding how these collaborations work, your nonprofit can use cause-related marketing to really get your message out there and bring in more support for your cause.

How Do I Partner with Businesses for More Cause-Related Marketing?

Nonprofits can forge impactful cause-related marketing partnerships with businesses by strategically aligning mutual goals, values, and audiences. Here's how nonprofits can approach and cultivate these beneficial relationships:

Identify Alignment in Mission and Values

Begin by identifying businesses that share similar values or have a vested interest in your cause. A genuine alignment between a nonprofit's mission and a business's corporate social responsibility goals lays a strong foundation for a meaningful partnership. Research potential partners to understand their brand ethos, past charitable initiatives, and how they engage with their customers and the community.

Develop a Compelling Proposal

Create a well-crafted proposal that clearly outlines the benefits of the partnership for the business, such as enhanced brand reputation, increased customer loyalty, and positive PR opportunities. Emphasize how the partnership can help the business reach new audiences or deepen its connection with existing ones. Provide concrete examples of how your nonprofit has successfully engaged supporters and the impact you've made, demonstrating your capacity to deliver value.

Create Co-Branded Campaigns

Collaborate with your business partner to develop co-branded marketing campaigns. These campaigns should resonate with the values and interests of both your nonprofit's supporters and the business's customers. Effective co-branded campaigns can range from special product offerings where a portion of the proceeds goes to your nonprofit, to joint events, social media campaigns, or volunteer initiatives. Ensure that the campaign messaging is consistent and authentically represents both parties.

Leverage Each Other's Strengths

Utilize the strengths of each partner for mutual benefit. Nonprofits can offer deep insights into the cause, stories of impact, and access to a dedicated supporter base. Businesses, on the other hand, can provide marketing expertise, financial resources, and a broad customer base. Collaborate closely to ensure that each partner's assets are effectively leveraged in the campaign.

Ensure Transparency and Accountability

Maintain transparency throughout the partnership, especially in terms of how funds are raised and used. Clear communication about the impact of the partnership not only builds trust but also reinforces the credibility of both the nonprofit and the business. Regularly update each other and your respective audiences on the partnership's progress and the tangible outcomes of the joint initiatives.

Evaluate and Celebrate Success

After the campaign, evaluate the results against the objectives set at the beginning of the partnership. Assess metrics such as funds raised, awareness generated, and engagement levels. Celebrate the successes and share the achievements with your supporters and the business's customers. Use the insights gained from the campaign to refine future initiatives and strengthen the partnership.

By approaching cause-related marketing partnerships thoughtfully and strategically, nonprofits can unlock powerful opportunities to advance their mission, increase their impact, and build enduring relationships with the business sector.

Trend 14: Rise of Social Media Influencers in Fundraising

Mr. Beast, a YouTube personality, has raised almost $600,000 to fund 100 wells in Cameroon, Kenya, Somalia, Uganda, and Zimbabwe.[viii] He also distributes food (14 million pounds of food to date), funded an orphanage, and brought solar power to villages in Zambia.

High-profile influencers like Mr. Beast, Tim Tebow, and Leonardo DiCaprio not only contribute their own resources to causes such as clean water initiatives and hunger relief but also inspire their vast followings to support these missions. This trend predicts that the trend of influencers championing charitable causes will not only continue but intensify in 2024, opening new avenues for nonprofits to collaborate with these digital powerhouses.

We'll explore the growing phenomenon of influencer-led fundraising, examining how the authenticity and reach of influencers like Mr. Beast and Tim Tebow can be harnessed to create impactful fundraising campaigns. This trend discusses how nonprofits can identify and partner with influencers whose values and audience align with their mission, creating campaigns that resonate and drive engagement.

In 2024, it's predicted that an increasing number of celebrity influencers will venture into founding their own charities, motivated by a desire to make a positive impact on society.

However, this trend is expected to come with its own set of challenges. Successfully managing a charity requires a comprehensive understanding of the nonprofit sector, strong organizational skills, and a commitment to financial transparency, areas that may be new or challenging for some influencers. As a result, several of these newly established charities might struggle to meet their goals, with issues potentially arising from mismanagement of funds or underestimating the complexities involved in running a charitable organization. This anticipated trend underscores the importance of thorough preparation, expert guidance, and diligent oversight in the charitable initiatives led by influencers to ensure that their efforts are both effective and sustainable.

How Do I Work with Influencers for Charitable Campaigns?

Nonprofit organizations can significantly benefit from collaborating with influencers in their fundraising campaigns, leveraging the influencers' reach and appeal to garner support and donations. However, this partnership must be navigated thoughtfully to maximize benefits and mitigate potential risks. Here's how nonprofits can effectively engage influencers in their fundraising efforts, along with the challenges they might face:

Strategic Selection of Influencers

Nonprofits should meticulously select influencers whose values align with their mission and whose followers are likely to resonate with their cause. This alignment ensures that the influencer's advocacy feels authentic and genuine, increasing the likelihood of positive engagement. Conducting thorough research into the influencer's past collaborations, audience demographics, and engagement patterns is crucial for a fruitful partnership.

Clear and Transparent Collaboration Agreements

It's essential for nonprofits to establish clear and transparent collaboration agreements with influencers. These agreements should outline the expectations, roles, and responsibilities of both parties, including the specifics of the campaign, the messaging guidelines, and the desired outcomes. Clear communication from the outset can prevent misunderstandings and ensure that both the influencer and the nonprofit are working towards a common goal.

Leveraging the Influencer's Creative Strengths

Influencers are adept at creating content that resonates with their audience. Nonprofits should harness this creative strength, allowing influencers to craft compelling narratives around the cause while ensuring that the core message and facts remain accurate. Authentic, engaging content produced by influencers can significantly boost campaign visibility and donor engagement.

Monitoring and Measuring Impact

Nonprofits should closely monitor the campaign's progress and measure its impact. Metrics such as engagement rates, donation amounts, and new supporter acquisition can provide valuable insights into the campaign's effectiveness. This data not only informs the current campaign's strategy but also aids in refining future influencer collaborations.

Challenges and Reputational Risk Management

While partnering with influencers offers numerous benefits, it also presents challenges, particularly concerning reputational risk. Influencers are public figures, and any negative press or controversy surrounding them can potentially impact the nonprofit's reputation. To mitigate this risk, nonprofits should:

- Conduct thorough background checks on potential influencer partners, assessing their public image and any past controversies.

- Establish crisis management plans to address potential negative situations swiftly and effectively.
- Maintain a diversified fundraising strategy, ensuring that the organization is not overly reliant on a single influencer or campaign.

Engaging influencers in fundraising campaigns can offer nonprofits a powerful platform to amplify their message and mobilize resources. However, it's crucial for organizations to approach these collaborations strategically, focusing on alignment, clear communication, creative freedom, impact measurement, and risk management. With careful planning and execution, partnerships with influencers can yield significant benefits, driving success in fundraising campaigns and advancing the nonprofit's mission.

Trend 15: Adoption of Subscription Model Donations

Recurring giving has been a giving trend for the last several years and we predict it will continue to grow in 2024. However, monthly donor acquisition will be challenging and expensive in 2024. Nonprofits that embrace recurring giving while improving donor experience will succeed in 2024.

As we look towards 2024, the importance of establishing and maintaining a base of monthly donors is more evident than ever.

"In a subscription friendly culture," Mike Meyers, fundraising leader, said, "monthly giving is a great place to invest."

However, amidst this growth, nonprofits are faced with the significant challenges of attracting and retaining these monthly contributors in an increasingly competitive landscape.

We will explore effective strategies for engaging monthly donors, emphasizing the importance of an exceptional donor experience. Nonprofits must focus on nurturing long-term relationships with their supporters by offering meaningful interactions and transparent communications. A key component of this relationship-building involves impactful reporting – demonstrating in a clear and compelling way how each donation is making a difference. By making donors feel informed and valued, nonprofits can foster loyalty and encourage continued support.

This trend also addresses the challenges of acquiring new monthly donors cost-effectively. We'll discuss leveraging digital marketing, compelling storytelling, and community engagement as vital tools in attracting new supporters. Recognizing and adapting to the changing preferences and behaviors of donors is essential in this dynamic environment.

In navigating the future of recurring giving, Trend 15 provides a comprehensive guide for nonprofits to not only adapt to the evolving landscape but to thrive within it. By prioritizing donor experience, transparency in impact reporting, and innovative acquisition strategies, nonprofits can build a strong foundation of sustained support, crucial for achieving long-term success and making a lasting impact.

How to Grow Subscription Giving in 2024

To grow recurring giving in 2024, nonprofits must prioritize personalized engagement with their donors. Understanding donor preferences, history, and behavior is key to tailoring communications and interactions. Use data analytics to segment your donor base and create personalized messaging that resonates with each group. Regular, meaningful communication that acknowledges each donor's unique contribution can foster a deeper connection and encourage ongoing support. Personal touches like birthday messages, anniversary acknowledgments of their first donation, and updates directly related to the aspects of the cause they care most about can make all the difference.

Leveraging Technology for Seamless Donations

In 2024, the seamless integration of technology in the donation process will be crucial for encouraging recurring giving. Nonprofits should invest in user-friendly, secure platforms that make the donation process as straightforward and hassle-free as possible. Features like easy-to-navigate donation pages, multiple payment options, and the ability to manage and update donation amounts independently can enhance the donor experience. Many nonprofit organizations are moving towards user-friendly donation form systems like FundraiseUp or iDonate. These tools also help increase the number of recurring givers by upselling donors to monthly giving. Automated email confirmations, receipts, and reminders for upcoming donations can also help in maintaining transparency and trust with your donors.

"Nonprofits must have an operational plan in place before promoting their monthly giving program," explained Mike Meyers. "You don't want to spend a lot of money acquiring donors if they're walking out the back door. Create great processes to ensure you keep the donors you acquire."

Implementing Effective Stewardship Programs

Stewardship is about nurturing and maintaining relationships with your donors. Implementing effective stewardship programs can play a significant role in growing recurring giving. At World Concern, we've adapted our monthly giving program, One Village, to focus more on the donor experience and provide resources that engage donors. We've also revamped how we acquired monthly donors by including more events. This has led to a 25% growth in monthly donors year over year. Create programs that recognize and reward recurring donors, perhaps through exclusive updates, special events, or recognition on your website or annual reports. Regularly express gratitude and show donors the tangible impact of their contributions, reinforcing the value and importance of their continued support.

Creating a Community of Recurring Donors

Building a community among your recurring donors can lead to a more engaged and committed supporter base. Consider creating exclusive groups or forums where recurring donors can interact, share experiences, and feel part of a larger collective impact. Highlight stories of individual donors and the difference their contributions are making. Encouraging this sense of community can turn individual donors into advocates for your cause, potentially attracting more recurring supporters through their networks.

Adapting to Donor Feedback

In 2024, adapting to donor feedback will be essential for retaining and growing your base of recurring donors. Regularly seek and listen to feedback about the donation process, communication preferences, and the overall donor experience. Be prepared to make changes based on this feedback. Showing that you value and act upon donor input can strengthen relationships and encourage donors to continue their support.

By prioritizing personalized engagement, leveraging technology for a seamless donation experience, implementing effective stewardship programs, fostering a donor community, and adapting to feedback, nonprofits can significantly grow their recurring giving in 2024. These strategies not only enhance the donor experience but also build a strong, loyal base of supporters committed to the long-term success of your cause.

Part 4: Impact & Accountability

During times of economic uncertainty, donors often cut the number of nonprofit organizations they support. If they normally give to 3-5 organizations, they may narrow that down to the 2-3 organizations that they love.

In Part 4, we look at critical trends shaping how nonprofits manage and communicate their effectiveness and adherence to best practices in 2024. This section is dedicated to exploring the nuances of donor privacy, the importance of transparent impact reporting, and the growing demands of regulation and compliance. As the nonprofit sector evolves, these trends reflect a broader shift towards greater transparency, accountability, and ethical stewardship in all facets of operations.

Trend 16: Increased Focus on Donor Privacy

In 2024, donor privacy takes center stage. With digital data becoming an invaluable asset, nonprofits are recognizing the imperative need to protect donor information. This trend highlights the increasing expectations of donors regarding the security and privacy of their data. Nonprofits are adopting robust data protection measures, implementing advanced security protocols, and ensuring compliance with data protection regulations. This trend will guide organizations through the complexities of data privacy, offering strategies to build trust with donors by safeguarding their personal information and being transparent about data usage.

Trend 17: Transparent Impact Reporting

The demand for transparent impact reporting is more pronounced than ever in 2024. Donors are not just giving; they want to know how their contributions are making a difference. This trend emphasizes the significance of clear, honest, and compelling communication about the outcomes and impact of nonprofit initiatives. We'll explore how organizations can leverage data, storytelling, and innovative reporting tools to convey the tangible results of their work. Transparent impact reporting not only satisfies donor curiosity but also strengthens donor relationships, enhances credibility, and fosters a culture of accountability.

Trend 18: Increased Regulation and Compliance

As the sector grows, so does the scrutiny it faces. In 2024, nonprofits are navigating an increasingly complex regulatory landscape. This trend underscores the importance of understanding and adhering to the myriad of regulations and standards governing the sector. From financial reporting to fundraising practices, compliance is not just a legal requirement but a fundamental aspect of operational integrity and donor trust. This trend will provide insights into staying ahead of regulatory changes, maintaining compliance, and embedding a culture of ethical practice across all organizational levels.

Part 4 of this book is a deep dive into the core elements of impact and accountability that are shaping the nonprofit sector in 2024. By focusing on donor privacy, transparent impact reporting, and adherence to regulation and compliance, nonprofits are not just responding to external demands but are proactively leading the way in setting new standards for integrity, transparency, and effectiveness in the pursuit of their missions.

Trend 16: Increased Focus on Donor Privacy

In the EU and UK, privacy regulations have dramatically changed how nonprofit organizations can interact with prospects and donors. We predict that 2024 will see an expansion of donor privacy initiatives in the United States.

In 2024, as digital interactions become the norm and data emerges as a crucial asset, the safeguarding of donor information is not just a preference but a necessity. This trend reflects a heightened awareness and concern among donors regarding the privacy and security of their personal data. It underscores the critical responsibility of nonprofits to not only protect this sensitive information but also to cultivate an environment of trust and transparency around their data practices.

In this section, we'll explore the multifaceted dimensions of donor privacy, from understanding the legal requirements and ethical considerations to implementing robust data protection measures. We'll explore the best practices for managing and securing donor data, ensuring compliance with evolving data protection regulations, and effectively communicating these practices to donors.

One challenge for nonprofits to overcome with data privacy: there is not a single regulation or law to follow, each state sets their own standards. In the past three years, 11 states adopted comprehensive data privacy laws. Colorado and Oregon offer no nonprofit exemptions, while other states' exemptions for nonprofits are less than you might expect.[ix]

Donors are going to require nonprofits they support to safeguard their information. As we navigate through this trend, we'll uncover the strategies and tools that nonprofits can employ not just to meet but exceed expectations in this critical area of donor privacy.

Focus on Donor Privacy

The protection of donor data is not just a legal obligation but a cornerstone of maintaining trust and credibility with supporters. Nonprofits must recognize that every piece of donor information they collect is a testament to the trust placed in them by their supporters. Safeguarding this data is paramount to preserving this trust and ensuring the privacy and security of their donors.

Establishing Strong Data Protection Policies

The first step in safeguarding donor data is to establish comprehensive data protection policies. These policies should outline how donor data is collected, stored, used, and shared. They should also define the roles and responsibilities of team members in handling and protecting data. Regularly reviewing and updating these policies in line with the latest data protection laws and best practices is essential.

Investing in Secure Technology

Investing in technology that prioritizes data security is crucial for nonprofits. This includes using secure, encrypted databases for storing donor information and ensuring that any third-party platforms or services used also adhere to high data protection standards. Regularly updating systems, employing firewalls, and using anti-malware software can further fortify the organization against data breaches.

Training and Awareness for Staff and Volunteers

A significant aspect of safeguarding donor data involves educating staff and volunteers about the importance of data privacy and the specific measures in place to protect it. Regular training sessions should be conducted to ensure everyone is aware of the best practices for handling donor information, recognizing potential threats, and responding to data breaches.

Staying Informed on Data Protection Regulations

Nonprofits need to stay informed about the data protection regulations applicable in their region, such as the GDPR in Europe or the CCPA in California. Understanding these regulations and ensuring compliance is not just about avoiding penalties but also about demonstrating a commitment to donor privacy.

Regularly Assessing and Improving Data Protection Practices

Conducting regular audits of data protection practices helps identify potential vulnerabilities and areas for improvement. Nonprofits should assess how data is collected, stored, accessed, and disposed of, making necessary adjustments to enhance security. Engaging with data protection experts or consultants can provide additional insights and recommendations.

Being Transparent about Data Practices

Transparency about data practices is key to building and maintaining trust with donors. Nonprofits should clearly communicate their data protection policies, how donor data is used, and the rights of donors regarding their data. This information should be easily accessible, for instance, through the organization's website or donor communication materials.

Responding Effectively to Data Breaches

Having a clear response plan is crucial in the unfortunate event of a data breach. Nonprofits should be prepared to act swiftly to secure data, assess the extent of the breach, and communicate openly with affected donors. An effective response mitigates the damage and demonstrates the organization's commitment to donor privacy and transparency.

Safeguarding donor data involves strong policies, secure technology, informed staff, legal compliance, and transparent communication. By prioritizing these aspects, nonprofits can protect their donors' data effectively, maintaining the trust and confidence that is essential for a successful and sustainable supporter relationship.

Trend 17: Transparent Impact Reporting

Donors are not just content with giving. They want to see and understand the real-world impact of their contributions. This trend emphasizes the growing demand for openness, accountability, and clear communication from nonprofits regarding how funds are used and the tangible outcomes achieved.

In this trend, we explore how transparent impact reporting can significantly strengthen donor trust, loyalty, and the overall reputation of an organization. We'll discuss how to effectively convey the real-world impact of donations through clear, engaging reports. From utilizing data visualization to enhance comprehension to using storytelling to connect with donors emotionally, this trend focuses on transforming quantitative data into narratives that truly resonate with supporters.

Transparent impact reporting goes beyond fulfilling a requirement; it reflects a commitment to honesty, accountability, and continuous growth. As we journey through this trend, we'll highlight the methods and tools that empower nonprofits to clearly communicate their achievements, thereby deepening their relationships with donors and affirming their dedication to transparency and ethical practices.

In practice, transparent impact reporting involves nonprofits meticulously documenting and explaining how donor funds are utilized and the specific impacts achieved. For instance, a nonprofit could publish an annual impact report containing detailed statistics, success stories, and vivid photographs illustrating their progress. They might also use infographics to visually represent how each dollar is spent or provide interactive online platforms where donors can track the progress of specific projects in real-time.

Additionally, organizations could host virtual or in-person events where beneficiaries share firsthand accounts of how the donations have transformed their lives. These practices ensure that donors are not just informed but are also engaged and deeply connected to the tangible outcomes of their generosity.

How Does a Nonprofit Organization Become More Transparent?

To enhance transparency, nonprofits should implement a holistic strategy that encompasses all organizational facets. This strategy involves sharing detailed reports on financial health, program results, and governance practices. By providing a complete, clear overview of operations and progress, nonprofits ensure that stakeholders fully understand their work and impact.

Communicating Financials Clearly

Financial transparency is crucial. Nonprofits should present income, expenses, and fund allocations in a user-friendly format. Utilizing charts, graphs, and infographics can help simplify complex financial data, making it more digestible for a broader audience.

Storytelling for Impact

Transparency goes beyond numbers; it's about sharing the human side of your work. Nonprofits should use stories, case studies, and testimonials to vividly illustrate their impact. Personal stories create an emotional connection, bringing data to life and making your impact tangible and relatable to donors.

Leveraging Technology for Engagement

Adopting digital tools can provide dynamic, real-time insights into your work. Interactive dashboards, maps, and apps offer an engaging way for donors to see the direct results of their contributions, enhancing transparency and donor engagement.

Encouraging Dialogue and Regular Updates

Transparency involves two-way communication. Nonprofits should actively engage with donors, offering platforms for feedback and conducting regular surveys. Regular updates and open Q&A sessions demonstrate an organization's commitment to transparency and accountability.

By adopting these practices, nonprofits can build trust, engage donors more effectively, and establish a culture of transparency that supports their mission and growth.

Trend 18: Increased Regulation and Compliance

In the face of stricter regulation and compliance, nonprofits are presented with a unique opportunity: to transform these challenges based on a commitment to transparency and integrity, thereby strengthening trust and deepening the impact of their mission.

This year, the sector faces increased scrutiny, with a growing emphasis on maintaining high standards of accountability, transparency, and ethical operation. This trend reflects the pressing need for nonprofits to keep pace with stricter regulatory requirements, ensuring their practices align with the evolving standards of governance and public trust.

In this section, we'll break down the complexities of this regulatory shift and what it means for nonprofits. We'll guide you through understanding and adhering to the latest legal and compliance demands, covering various operational aspects from fundraising to financial reporting.

This trend indicates a broader call for organizations to uphold a strong commitment to ethical practices and responsible management. We'll explore how nonprofits can effectively tackle these regulatory challenges, maintain solid compliance frameworks, and foster a culture that prioritizes openness and integrity. Dive into this critical discussion as we examine the essential role of regulation and compliance in shaping the responsible and impactful future of the nonprofit sector.

How Does Your Nonprofit Operate in an Increasingly Regulated Environment?

The first step for a nonprofit in adapting to increased regulation is to gain a thorough understanding of the current regulatory landscape. Nonprofits should stay informed about the latest laws, guidelines, and standards that affect their operations. This involves not only being aware of national regulations but also understanding local and international laws if the organization operates across borders. Regularly consulting with legal experts, attending workshops, and subscribing to regulatory updates can ensure that your nonprofit stays ahead of the curve.

Prioritizing Compliance in Organizational Culture

To thrive in an environment of increased regulation, nonprofits must prioritize compliance at every level of the organization. This means fostering a culture where compliance is seen as integral to the mission, not just a legal necessity. Staff and volunteers should be trained and encouraged to understand the importance of regulations and how they relate to their daily activities. Establishing clear, organization-wide policies and ensuring that everyone is aware of and committed to these guidelines will create a proactive, compliance-first culture.

Implementing Effective Compliance Tools and Systems

Nonprofits should invest in the right tools and systems to manage compliance effectively. This may involve adopting software for tracking and reporting financial transactions, donor management systems that ensure data privacy, or project management tools that help monitor program outcomes against regulatory standards. Regular audits and checks should be part of the routine to ensure that these systems are functioning correctly and that the organization remains compliant.

Identifying and Mitigating Compliance Risks

Proactive risk management is crucial in an environment of increased regulation. Nonprofits should regularly assess potential compliance risks and develop strategies to mitigate them. This involves understanding the areas of operation that are most at risk of non-compliance, such as financial reporting or donor data privacy, and putting in place preventive measures. Regular risk assessments and a clear protocol for addressing any issues that arise will help ensure that the organization remains on the right side of regulations.

Fostering Transparency with Stakeholders

Transparency is key in an environment of increased regulation. Nonprofits should maintain open lines of communication with donors, supporters, and regulatory bodies. This includes not only reporting on financials and program outcomes but also being transparent about compliance efforts and any challenges faced. By openly sharing their compliance journey, nonprofits can build trust and demonstrate their commitment to operating with integrity and accountability.

Adapting to increased regulation involves understanding the regulatory environment, building a compliance-first culture, investing in robust systems, engaging in proactive risk management, and maintaining transparent communication. By taking these steps, nonprofits can not only ensure compliance but also strengthen their operations and enhance the trust and confidence of their stakeholders.

Part 5: Macro Trends

In Part 5, "Macro Trends," we examine the broader societal and organizational shifts shaping the nonprofit sector's landscape in 2024. These trends capture the pulse of the times, reflecting the interplay between societal dynamics, political climates, and organizational behaviors. From the impact of presidential elections on donor behavior to the implications of changing religious attendance patterns, and from the strategic moves of mergers and consolidations to the rise of 'rage giving' and the focus on localizing grant funding, this section dissects the factors that are redefining the parameters of nonprofit operations and fundraising. Additionally, we address the critical issue of staff turnover, analyzing its causes and effects within the sector. As we navigate these macro trends, we uncover the challenges and opportunities they present, offering insights and strategies for nonprofits to adapt and thrive in a rapidly evolving environment.

Trend 19: Impact of Presidential Elections

The presidential election years often bring a climate of uncertainty and volatility, influencing donor priorities and behaviors. In this trend, we explore how election outcomes and political climates can affect fundraising efforts, shifting the focus of donors and potentially impacting the flow of donations to various causes.

Trend 20: Decline in Church Attendance Affecting Giving

As church attendance continues to decline, its traditional role in driving charitable giving is also changing. This trend delves into how this shift is impacting philanthropy, particularly for faith-based and community-focused nonprofits, and how these organizations can adapt to a changing donor base.

Trend 21: Mergers & Consolidations

In response to the increasing pressures for efficiency and impact, more nonprofits are considering mergers and consolidations. This trend examines the strategic considerations behind these decisions, the challenges and benefits of merging operations, and how these moves can reshape the nonprofit landscape.

Trend 22: Protests & Increase in 'Rage Giving'

In times of social and political unrest, the phenomenon of 'rage giving'—donating as an immediate response to controversial events or policies—gains prominence. This trend analyzes how nonprofits can navigate this reactive form of giving, ensuring that it translates into sustained support and engagement.

Trend 23: Shift Grant Funding to Localization

There's a growing emphasis on localizing grant funding, focusing on community-driven solutions and grassroots organizations. This trend explores the implications of this shift for larger nonprofits and how they can foster local partnerships and initiatives to align with this more localized approach to funding.

Trend 24: Staff Turnover

Staff turnover remains a critical issue in the nonprofit sector, affecting continuity, institutional knowledge, and morale. In this trend, we examine the underlying causes of high turnover rates and offer strategies for nonprofits to attract, retain, and nurture talent, fostering a stable and committed workforce.

In Part 5, we navigate through these macro trends, understanding their nuances and preparing for their implications. By staying informed and adaptive, nonprofits can position themselves to effectively respond to these broader societal and organizational shifts, turning potential challenges into opportunities for growth and impact.

Trend 19: Impact of Presidential Elections

P residential election years can be a significant challenge for non-political nonprofit organizations. It's not just the flow of money to the political campaigns, it's the fear that each side tries to instill in donors that can hold them back from making any serious financial commitments, even to nonprofit organizations.

Presidential election years are known for their unique dynamics, characterized by heightened public discourse, shifting priorities, and economic uncertainties. These factors collectively play a significant role in shaping donor attitudes and behaviors, making it a critical period for nonprofits to navigate.

In this section, we explore how the fervor and polarization often associated with presidential elections can impact the philanthropic climate. Election years can consciousness. Craft your messages to demonstrate the relevance and urgency of your work. Use storytelling to highlight the tangible impact of donations, making it clear how supporting your cause can lead to positive change amid the broader political landscape.

Leveraging Technology and Social Media

Utilize technology and social media to keep your cause visible and engaging. Digital platforms offer a cost-effective way to reach and mobilize your audience. Tailor your online content to be shareable and relevant to current discussions, ensuring that your organization remains part of the conversation during the election period. Online fundraising campaigns, virtual events, and interactive social media initiatives can keep your supporters involved and motivated to contribute.

Maintaining Transparency and Building Trust

During a presidential election year, maintaining transparency and building trust are more important than ever. Clearly communicate how funds are being used and the impact they're making. Donors are more likely to continue supporting your cause if they feel confident about the integrity and effectiveness of your organization. Regular updates, impact reports, and testimonials can reinforce the value of your work and the importance of ongoing support.

Preparing for Post-Election Engagement

Finally, it's important to have a plan for post-election engagement. Once the election is over, there may be opportunities to reconnect with donors whose attention was diverted. Review the outcomes of the election and adjust your messaging and strategies accordingly. Continue to emphasize the importance of your cause and the difference that continued support can make in the lives of those you serve.

By anticipating shifts, adjusting strategies, engaging donors compellingly, leveraging digital tools, maintaining transparency, and preparing for post-election engagement, your nonprofit can navigate the challenges of a presidential election year and continue to drive its mission forward.

Trend 20: Decline in Church Attendance Affecting Giving

The dechurching trend in America is having a much wider impact beyond religious institutions. It's estimated that forty million adults (16%) of American adults have quit the church over the past twenty-five years.[x] This trend is reshaping the landscape of philanthropy, particularly impacting how and why individuals contribute to charitable causes.

Historically, churches and religious organizations have played a crucial role in promoting a culture of giving. As their impact wanes, nonprofits face both challenges and opportunities. This trend could affect charitable contributions, regardless of whether your organization is affiliated with a religious institution. We will explore the reasons behind this shift, how it might alter donation trends, and the ways nonprofits can adjust their strategies to meet the changing needs and preferences of donors.

In addressing this trend, our goal is to offer practical guidance to help nonprofits successfully manage these changes. By comprehending and adapting to the evolving landscape of faith-based giving, organizations can maintain strong connections with their supporters and keep the spirit of philanthropy alive even as societal attitudes shift.

How Should Nonprofit Organizations Deal with a Decline in Church Attendance?

As church attendance declines, nonprofits must first seek to understand how this trend is affecting traditional giving patterns. This involves analyzing data and gathering insights into the motivations and preferences of donors who previously gave through religious channels. Recognizing that these individuals may still be inclined to give, but perhaps through different avenues or for different reasons, is key to adapting your outreach and engagement strategies.

Expanding Beyond Traditional Venues

With the decline in church attendance, nonprofits need to diversify their fundraising channels to reach potential donors. This means exploring and investing in various platforms and methods, such as digital fundraising, community events, and peer-to-peer campaigns. Embracing a multi-channel approach allows organizations to cast a wider net and engage donors in spaces where they are now more likely to be active.

Enhancing Online Presence and Engagement

In today's digital-first environment, having a strong online presence is crucial. Nonprofits should focus on building and maintaining an engaging website, active social media profiles, and an impactful content strategy. These digital assets are invaluable for reaching a broader audience, sharing compelling stories, and making it easy for supporters to learn about your cause and contribute online.

Building New Communities of Support

As the role of church communities in fostering giving

shifts, nonprofits can focus on building new communities around shared values and causes. Hosting community events, volunteer opportunities, and discussion forums can help create a sense of belonging and collective purpose, similar to what individuals might have experienced within a religious community.

This is especially vital for the religious-affiliated nonprofits. It's estimated these organizations compose 40% of the social safety net in America.[xi] These organizations must look beyond the walls of the church for financial and volunteer support.

Emphasizing Shared Values and Impact

"The age of institutional giving is gone," explained Jess Rainer, Pastor and Author of *How to Launch a New Church Site*. "Non-profit organizations must provide compelling reasons that motivate the hearts of givers."

Nonprofits should articulate and emphasize the shared values that resonate with their audience. Communicating the tangible impact of contributions and how they align with the broader values and goals of your supporters can help bridge the gap left by declining church attendance. Showcasing success stories and the real-world impact of donations fosters a deep connection and a sense of shared accomplishment.

Engaging Younger Generations

As younger generations show different patterns of religious engagement and giving, nonprofits must tailor their strategies to meet these changes. Understanding the preferences, communication styles, and values of younger donors is crucial. Nonprofits should adapt their messaging, use the right channels for outreach, and offer various ways for these donors to engage with and support the cause.

Dealing with the decline in church attendance requires nonprofits to thoroughly understand the evolving landscape, diversify their fundraising channels, enhance their online engagement, foster new communities of support, and adapt to generational changes. By taking these proactive steps, organizations can continue to inspire generosity and sustain their impactful work, even amidst shifting social dynamics.

Trend 21: Mergers & Consolidations

This year could be poised for an unprecedented wave of mergers and acquisitions, driven by strategic alignments among nonprofits and a significant shift within fundraising agencies as their founders approach retirement age. This trend is reshaping the structural fabric of the sector, prompting organizations to reevaluate their strategies and consider the potential benefits and implications of merging.

In this section, we explore the factors contributing to this surge in mergers and acquisitions. For nonprofits, merging with another organization can be a strategic move to amplify impact, share resources, and enhance service delivery. A 2012 study of 41 nonprofit mergers found that organizations merge to increase service delivery (93%), strategic vision for mergers (66%), or to improve financial stability (61%).[xii] However, it also involves complex considerations regarding mission alignment, organizational culture, and operational integration.

In January 2024, Childhaven and Children's Home Society of Washington (CHSW) merged to form Akin, a new entity aimed at innovating and enhancing social services for lifelong family well-being in Washington state. Akin CEO Dave Newell said, "This merger allows us to grow and evolve as one organization, not for the sake of size but for the scope of direct impact in how Akin can partner with parents, caregivers, children and communities, together, to strengthen families."[xiii]

Simultaneously, the fundraising agency landscape is experiencing its own transformation. As agency founders retire, the resulting acquisitions and mergers are leading to a reshuffling of partnerships and services. Nonprofits must navigate these changes carefully, assessing how a different or newly merged agency might affect their fundraising strategies, relationships, and overall success.

Just in the past two years, we've seen:

- Allegiance Group and Pursuant Group merged
- One & All Agency acquired by TrueSense Marketing
- Nonprofit Operating System acquired by iWave
- Classy acquired by GoFundMe
- Mission + Strategy Consulting acquired by Keystone Alliance

Throughout this trend, we'll provide insights into the decision-making process for nonprofits contemplating a merger, and offer guidance on managing the transition of fundraising agency partnerships. Understanding the landscape of consolidation in 2024 is crucial for nonprofits to make informed decisions, adapt to the evolving sector, and continue to thrive in their mission-driven endeavors.

How Should Your Nonprofit Navigate 2024 If You're Looking to Merge with Another Nonprofit?

Before exploring a merger, it's crucial to conduct

thorough due diligence. This involves a comprehensive assessment of the potential partner organization's financial health, operational efficiency, legal obligations, and cultural fit. Understanding these aspects in detail helps in identifying any potential risks or challenges that could arise post-merger. It's also important to evaluate how the merger aligns with your nonprofit's strategic goals and mission, ensuring that the partnership will strengthen, rather than dilute, your organization's impact.

Evaluating Mission and Cultural Alignment

A successful merger goes beyond financial and operational alignment; it requires a deep synergy between the missions and cultures of the merging organizations. Assess the core values, work cultures, and operational philosophies of both entities. The goal is to ensure that the merged organization can function as a cohesive unit, with a shared vision and a harmonious work environment. Engaging in open discussions about organizational cultures, expectations, and future goals is key to establishing a solid foundation for the merger.

Communicating Transparently with Stakeholders

Open and transparent communication with all stakeholders, including employees, donors, beneficiaries, and board members, is vital throughout the merger process. Keeping stakeholders informed about the intentions, potential benefits, and expected outcomes of the merger helps in building trust and ensuring a smooth transition. It's also important to provide a platform for stakeholders to voice their concerns, questions, and suggestions. This two-way communication can provide valuable insights and help in addressing any issues proactively.

Planning and Managing the Integration Process

Merging two organizations involves integrating various aspects of operations, including staff, systems, processes, and programs. Developing a detailed integration plan is crucial for a successful merger. This plan should outline the steps for combining operations, harmonizing policies, and unifying teams. It's also important to assign clear roles and responsibilities for managing the integration process and to establish timelines and milestones for tracking progress.

Seeking Expert Guidance and Support

Navigating a merger is a complex process that often requires specialized knowledge and expertise. Seeking guidance from legal advisors, financial consultants, and merger and acquisition experts can provide valuable support in making informed decisions and managing the technical aspects of the process. These professionals can offer insights into legal compliance, financial structuring, and change management, ensuring that the merger is executed smoothly and successfully.

Navigating a potential merger in 2024 requires careful planning, thorough due diligence, alignment in mission and culture, transparent communication with stakeholders, meticulous management of the integration process, and seeking expert advice. By addressing these key areas, your nonprofit can navigate the consolidation wave effectively, making strategic decisions that enhance your impact and ensure long-term sustainability.

What Should Your Nonprofit Do If Your Fundraising Agency is a Part of a Merger?

When your fundraising agency is involved in a merger, the first step is to assess how this change might impact your nonprofit. Understand the motives behind the merger, the new structure of the agency, and any potential shifts in services or strategies. Analyze whether the merger could lead to enhanced services, broader expertise, or access to more extensive networks that could benefit your fundraising efforts. Conversely, consider any possible disruptions or shifts in focus that may not align with your nonprofit's needs.

Evaluating Service Continuity and Quality

Post-merger, it's essential to evaluate whether the quality and continuity of the services provided by the agency will be maintained. Pay close attention to any changes in the agency's staff, particularly those who directly manage your account or projects. A change in key personnel could affect the quality of service or the understanding of your organization's unique needs.

Openly communicate your expectations and requirements to ensure that the service level and quality you expect are consistently met.

Reviewing Contractual Agreements and Terms

A merger can lead to changes in contractual agreements and terms of service. Review your current contract with the agency to understand your rights and any clauses that may be affected by the merger. It's advisable to consult with legal experts to navigate these changes and to discuss any necessary adjustments or renegotiations of terms. Ensure that your organization's interests are protected and that the terms of the partnership remain favorable.

Engaging in Open Dialogue with the Merged Entity

Establishing open lines of communication with the newly merged entity is crucial. Engage in discussions to understand their vision, the anticipated changes, and how they plan to serve your nonprofit moving forward. Express any concerns or questions you may have and seek clarity on aspects such as strategic direction, service offerings, and pricing. A transparent and open dialogue can help in building a strong partnership with the merged agency.

Monitoring Performance and Considering Alternatives

After the merger, closely monitor the performance and outcomes of your collaboration with the agency. Evaluate if the partnership continues to meet your nonprofit's fundraising goals and expectations. If you observe a decline in performance or a misalignment with your organization's needs, it may be prudent to consider alternative options. Conducting a market review to understand other available services and agencies can provide insights into potential partnerships that may better align with your strategic objectives.

If your fundraising agency is part of a merger, it's important to assess the implications, evaluate service continuity, review contractual terms, engage in open communication, and monitor performance. Being proactive, informed, and adaptable will help your nonprofit navigate this change effectively, ensuring that your fundraising efforts remain robust and successful.

Trend 22: Protests & Increase in 'Rage Giving'

Some donors are driven by rage more than a desire to see someone helped. The 2024 political season will see a rise in 'rage giving' as donors seek to express their political views through giving to an organization they see as attacking their political enemies.

We aren't referring to the many great political advocacy nonprofit organizations or to the political candidates or parties themselves. When we discuss 'rage giving,' we are talking about the organizations that encourage violence as political discourse.

As the political climate intensifies, individuals on both sides of the spectrum are increasingly channeling their passions and frustrations into charitable donations. This trend reflects a broader shift in donor behavior, where giving is not just a measure of support but also an expression of protest or solidarity with causes that align with personal or political beliefs.

In this section, we explore how nonprofits can navigate this surge in 'rage giving,' understanding the motivations behind it and the potential it holds for driving significant support to organizations. We'll discuss the ethical considerations, the importance of maintaining mission alignment, and how to sustainably engage donors who are initially motivated by a reaction to current events.

As we navigate through Trend 22, we'll provide insights into capitalizing on this form of giving without compromising the organization's values or long-term goals. Understanding 'rage giving' is crucial for nonprofits aiming to harness this passionate form of support while fostering a culture of sustained and meaningful philanthropy beyond the election cycle.

How Can Non-Political Charities Navigate Rage Giving in 2024?

In 2024, non-political charities will witness a surge in 'rage giving,' where donors contribute impulsively in response to political or social events. While these donations are often directed towards organizations directly involved in these events, non-political charities must adeptly navigate this trend to maintain support and engagement. Understanding the underlying motivations and emotional dynamics of 'rage giving' is essential for charities to effectively adapt their strategies and ensure sustained support.

Reaffirming Commitment to Core Mission

Non-political charities should consistently reinforce their commitment to their core mission and values, especially during times of heightened 'rage giving' to other causes. Clear and consistent communication about the organization's non-partisan stance and long-term objectives is crucial. Charities need to articulate how their work continues to be relevant and impactful, ensuring donors understand the importance of their contributions beyond the immediate, emotionally charged context.

Engaging Donors with a Unifying Message

In the midst of 'rage giving', it's important for non-political charities to engage donors with a unifying message that transcends political divides. Focus on storytelling and impact reporting that highlights the universal appeal of your mission. Emphasize the positive change that every donation facilitates, regardless of the donor's political leanings. This approach can help maintain donor interest and support, even as attention is drawn to more politically charged causes.

Ethical Navigation and Donor Education

As donors react to current events, non-political charities must carefully navigate these waters, ensuring that any engagement or messaging does not inadvertently polarize their supporter base. It's also an opportune time to educate donors about the ongoing needs that the charity addresses, the effectiveness of their approach, and the lasting impact of their work. This education can help redirect some of the passion and urgency of 'rage giving' towards sustained support for your cause.

Strategizing for Long-Term Engagement

While 'rage giving' may temporarily shift the focus away from non-political charities, these organizations should strategize for long-term engagement and support.

Encourage recurring donations and foster community involvement, ensuring that your charity remains a prominent and respected option for donors. Regular updates about your work and its impact can remind donors of the enduring value of their support, encouraging them to stay involved beyond the election cycle.

In navigating 'rage giving' in 2024, non-political charities face the challenge of maintaining support amidst a climate of heightened emotional giving to other causes. By staying true to their mission, engaging donors with a unifying message, navigating ethical considerations carefully, and strategizing for long-term engagement, charities can effectively sustain and grow their support base, even in a politically charged environment.

Trend 23: Shift Grant Funding to Localization

In 2024, we are witnessing a pivotal transformation as major grant-distributing organizations, including entities like USAID, are increasingly directing their funds toward local partners rather than international NGOs. USAID is planning to shift at least 25% of its annual grant funding to local partners by the end of FY2025.[xiv] This trend reflects a growing belief in the value and effectiveness of empowering local communities and organizations to drive change from within.

In this section, we delve into the implications of this shift for large nonprofits and how it is reshaping their roles and strategies in the international development landscape. We'll discuss the importance of fostering strong local partnerships, understanding community needs, and building capacities at the grassroots level. This trend not only challenges large organizations to rethink their operational models but also presents an opportunity to collaborate more closely with local entities, ensuring that interventions are culturally relevant, sustainable, and aligned with local priorities.

In the United States, a similar trend is taking shape as grantors increasingly show a preference for working with smaller, local partners over larger, more distant organizations. This shift is driven by the recognition that local partners often possess a deeper understanding of the community's unique needs, challenges, and cultural nuances, enabling them to implement more effective and sustainable solutions. By directing funds towards these local entities, grantors are not only ensuring that resources are used more efficiently but also fostering a sense of ownership and empowerment within the communities, leading to more impactful and long-lasting change. This trend underscores the growing importance of community-driven approaches and the need for larger organizations to adapt by forming meaningful collaborations and supporting local capacities.

How Do Nonprofit Organizations Navigate Localization Issues?

As funding increasingly shifts towards local entities, nonprofit organizations must adapt their strategies to remain relevant and impactful. This involves embracing the localization of funding, recognizing the value of local knowledge and community-driven approaches, and adjusting operational models accordingly.

Strengthening Local Partnerships and Capacity Building

Nonprofits should focus on forming and nurturing strong partnerships with local organizations. These relationships are crucial for understanding community needs and developing culturally appropriate solutions. By investing in capacity building, nonprofits can empower local partners, equipping them with the skills, knowledge, and resources necessary to lead and sustain initiatives. Supporting local partners not only enhances program effectiveness but also aligns with the preferences of funders who are increasingly looking to fund organizations with strong local ties.

Adapting Program Design and Implementation

Nonprofits must be willing to adapt their program design and implementation strategies to suit local contexts. This may involve decentralizing decision-making processes, involving community members in program planning, and being flexible and responsive to feedback and changing local needs. Programs that are designed and implemented with local insights are more likely to be accepted, effective, and sustainable.

Leveraging Local Expertise

Nonprofits should recognize and leverage the expertise of local staff and partners. These individuals bring invaluable insights into the community's social, cultural, and political dynamics. Involving local experts in program development, leadership roles, and decision-making ensures that interventions are relevant and resonate with the community's values and priorities.

Transparent Communication with Funders

Clear and transparent communication with funders about the importance and impact of local partnerships is essential. Nonprofits should articulate how working with local entities aligns with the funder's goals, leads to more effective use of resources, and contributes to sustainable development. Sharing success stories, challenges, and learnings from local partnerships can further demonstrate the value of localization to funders.

Monitoring, Evaluation, and Learning

Implementing robust monitoring and evaluation systems is crucial to assess the effectiveness of localized programs and partnerships. Nonprofits should use data and feedback to improve program design and implementation continuously. Additionally, documenting and sharing lessons learned from local collaborations can provide valuable insights for the organization, the community, and the broader sector.

Dealing with the trend towards localized funding requires nonprofits to embrace local partnerships, adapt their program strategies, leverage local expertise, communicate transparently with funders, and commit to continuous learning and improvement. By doing so, organizations can ensure that their initiatives are locally driven, contextually relevant, and aligned with the evolving preferences of donors and the communities they serve.

Trend 24: Staff Turnover

The average tenure of a development professional is alarmingly short, averaging just 16 months.[xv] This trend poses significant challenges for nonprofits, impacting their fundraising continuity, donor relationships, and overall organizational stability.

In this trend, we explore the multifaceted reasons behind this high turnover rate in fundraising roles. Factors such as excessive workload, unrealistic fundraising targets, lack of support from leadership, insufficient resources, and the emotional toll of constant engagement and solicitation contribute to burnout and job dissatisfaction. Additionally, the competitive nature of the sector often leads to poaching of talented professionals, further exacerbating the turnover problem.

Understanding the root causes of this turnover is crucial for nonprofits aiming to address and mitigate its impact. As we navigate through Trend 24, we'll provide insights into the strategies and practices that can help organizations retain their valuable development staff, foster a supportive work environment, and ultimately create a more stable and effective fundraising operation. Recognizing and tackling the issue of high turnover in fundraising roles is essential for the sustainability and success of nonprofits in fulfilling their missions.

Unrealistic Expectations and Workload

One of the primary reasons for high turnover in development roles is the set of unrealistic expectations often placed on fundraising professionals. Many are tasked with ambitious fundraising targets without the necessary resources or support. This imbalance can lead to a relentless workload, with development staff feeling the constant pressure to perform. The stress of meeting these high expectations, often with limited budget or personnel, can quickly lead to burnout, prompting individuals to seek relief by moving to other organizations or leaving the sector entirely.

Lack of Support and Recognition

Development professionals frequently face a lack of understanding and support from their organization's leadership and other departments. The unique challenges of fundraising are often underestimated, leading to a lack of recognition for the hard work and success of development teams. Without a supportive work environment that acknowledges their efforts and addresses their professional needs, development staff can feel undervalued and disheartened, fueling the desire to find a more appreciative and supportive workplace.

Limited Opportunities for Career Advancement

Many development professionals find themselves in a career standstill, with limited opportunities for growth or advancement within their organizations. The absence of clear career pathways or professional development opportunities can make the role feel stagnant. This lack of progression can drive development staff to seek advancement through external opportunities, contributing to the high turnover rate.

Emotional Toll and Donor Fatigue

Fundraising is inherently relational and often emotionally taxing. Development professionals invest significant emotional labor in building and maintaining donor relationships. The constant pressure to engage donors, coupled with the need to navigate the emotional highs and lows of fundraising campaigns, can take a considerable toll on an individual's well-being. Over time, this emotional burden can lead to donor fatigue, making the role unsustainable for many.

Competitive Market and Poaching

The nonprofit sector is highly competitive, and talented development professionals are in high demand. Organizations often resort to poaching staff from other nonprofits, offering better compensation, benefits, or work conditions. This competitive market creates an environment where development professionals are frequently presented with tempting offers from other organizations, leading to a higher turnover as individuals seek to improve their professional circumstances.

Addressing these factors is crucial for nonprofits planning to reduce turnover in development roles. By setting realistic expectations, providing ample support and recognition, offering clear career advancement opportunities, acknowledging the emotional aspects of the role, and creating a competitive and attractive work environment, organizations can foster loyalty and retain their valuable development staff.

How Does Your Nonprofit Retain Your Fundraising Staff?

"Nonprofit organizations may look at the laundry list that is encouraged in retaining talent and feel paralysis. Is each one warranted?" asked Brooke Hodnefield, VP Nonprofit for Slingshot Group. "Absolutely yes. But what is your organization's low-hanging fruit? If it can be prioritized by what your organization is already postured to do well…start there! Small, incremental changes with a recognition that 'we can and should do better,' as well as an authentic effort that is owned by leadership, can be a solid first step in the right direction. Just also consider that once you've declared it, you will be held accountable. What will take your retention in the opposite direction is to declare it and do nothing. Start small and sustain."

Fostering a Culture of Appreciation and Support

To retain fundraising staff, nonprofits must cultivate a work environment that values and supports its employees. Recognizing the hard work and achievements of fundraising professionals, both publicly and privately, can boost morale and job satisfaction. Regularly acknowledging their contributions and offering constructive feedback creates a positive work culture where staff feel valued and motivated.

Ensuring Realistic Goals and Work-Life Balance

Setting achievable fundraising targets and respecting the need for a healthy work-life balance are essential in retaining staff. Unrealistic expectations can lead to stress and burnout, so it's important to set goals that are challenging yet attainable, based on accurate data and the resources available. Encouraging staff to take time off and providing flexible work arrangements can also contribute to a more balanced and sustainable work environment.

Investing in Career Growth and Learning

Providing opportunities for professional development is key to retaining fundraising staff. Employees should have access to training, workshops, and conferences that can enhance their skills and knowledge. Establishing clear career pathways within the organization can also give staff a sense of direction and purpose, making them more likely to stay and grow with the nonprofit.

Enhancing Compensation and Benefits

Offering competitive salaries and comprehensive benefits is crucial in a competitive job market. Regularly review and adjust compensation packages to ensure they align with industry standards. Additionally, offering benefits like health insurance, retirement plans, and wellness programs can make your organization a more attractive and supportive place to work.

Encouraging Open Dialogue and Feedback

"As a leader within an organization, what is a powerful retention tool?" asked Brooke Hodnefield. "Truly listening and affirming what you've heard by what you say and what you do. When you invest in others...not just what they DO, but who they ARE, they feel valued.

"When your people feel valued, they deepen their personal investment, which in turn deepens their organizational investment. Sounds simple enough, but our frantic posture and hurried pace doesn't bode well for truly listening and being fully present with the people we lead. Great talent will often stay for great leadership, and for the investment they feel in who they are."

Maintaining open lines of communication between fundraising staff and leadership is vital. Create an environment where employees feel comfortable sharing their ideas, concerns, and feedback. Regular team meetings, one-on-one check-ins, and anonymous surveys can provide valuable insights into staff needs and help address any issues before they lead to turnover.

Recognizing and Addressing the Emotional Aspects of Fundraising

Acknowledge the emotional labor involved in fundraising and provide support systems to help staff manage the stresses of the job. Offering access to mental health resources, peer support groups, or counseling services can demonstrate your organization's commitment to the well-being of its employees.

Retaining fundraising staff requires a multifaceted approach that focuses on creating a supportive work environment, setting realistic goals, offering professional development opportunities, enhancing compensation and benefits, building strong internal communication, and recognizing the emotional aspects of fundraising. By addressing these areas, nonprofits can foster a positive, rewarding, and sustainable workplace that encourages staff to remain committed to their roles and the organization's mission.

End Notes

[i] https://thesignatry.com/blog/cash-isnt-really-king-noncash-contributions/
[ii] https://www.kiplinger.com/retirement/how-to-keep-your-wealth-transfer-on-track
[iii] https://www.schwabcharitable.org/resource/fiscal-year-2022-giving-report
[iv] https://www.nptechforgood.com/2023/08/04/6-generations-of-giving-who-gives-the-most-and-how-they-prefer-to-give/
[v] Ibid.
[vi] https://www.tiktok.com/for-good/
[vii] https://onestarfoundation.org/three-powerful-examples-of-government-nonprofit-collaboration-in-2021/
[viii] https://www.beastphilanthropy.org/
[ix] https://www.wagenmakerlaw.com/blog/2023-us-data-privacy-laws-impact-nonprofits
[x] https://www.thegospelcoalition.org/article/great-dechurching/
[xi] Ibid.
[xii] https://propelnonprofits.org/wp-content/uploads/2017/10/SuccessFactorsFullReport.pdf
[xiii] https://akinfamily.org/wp-content/uploads/2023/12/Akin_Merger_Release_FINAL_121523.pdf
[xiv] https://www.usaid.gov/localization
[xv] https://www.nonprofitpro.com/post/nonprofit-development-staff-turnover-is-it-a-crisis-or-an-old-paradigm-we-need-to-change/

About the Author

Jeremy Reis is the Vice President of Marketing for CRISTA Ministries, a family of ministries based in Seattle, Washington. At CRISTA, Jeremy manages the team responsible for marketing, creative, communications, monthly giving, direct mail, and digital fundraising for multiple ministries. Jeremy has worked in a variety of corporate, consulting, and nonprofit roles.

He started his career on the tech side and after finishing his MBA at The Ohio State University, jumped over to marketing with nonprofits. Jeremy is on the Advisory Council for Christian Leadership Alliance where he serves as a member of the strategy leadership.

Jeremy is the author of *Raise More Money with Email, Magnetic Nonprofit, 24 Fundraising Trends & Predictions for 2024,* and *Post-Pandemic Nonprofit*. He blogs at NonprofitFundraising.com and hosts the Nonprofit Answers podcast.

Elevate Your Fundraising

Unlock the full potential of your nonprofit with other books by **Jeremy Reis**, each crafted for different aspects of your organization's growth. Discover nonprofit growth secrets:

1. Magnetic Nonprofit: Attract and Retain Donors, Volunteers, and Staff

Transform your nonprofit to attract talent and resources. This book is a goldmine of strategies for creating an irresistible organization. Learn how to:

- **Attract Top Talent**: Discover methods to draw in passionate staff and volunteers.
- **Retain Donors**: Master the art of building lasting relationships with your donors.
- **Create a Magnetic Culture**: Develop a culture that inspires

commitment and enthusiasm.

2. Raise More Money with Email

Email is not just a communication tool; it's a fundraising powerhouse. In this insightful guide, you'll learn how to:

- **Craft Compelling Messages**: Engage your audience with emails they can't ignore.
- **Maximize Donations**: Use proven techniques to boost your email fundraising.
- **Build Stronger Connections**: Establish trust and rapport through effective email communication.

3. The Post-Pandemic Nonprofit: 12 Disruptive Trends Your Nonprofit Must Master

The pandemic changed the world, and nonprofits are no exception. Use this roadmap to navigate the new normal by:

- **Identifying Key Trends**: Stay ahead of the curve with insights into emerging trends.
- **Adapting to Change**: Learn how to pivot strategies in response to new challenges.
- **Thriving Post-Pandemic**: Equip your organization to succeed in the altered landscape.

These books are not just guides; they are blueprints for success. Elevate your nonprofit to new heights by mastering the art of attraction, communication, and adaptation in an ever-evolving world.

Order your copies at Amazon or other booksellers today and start transforming your nonprofit's future!

Made in the USA
Columbia, SC
11 February 2024